Maritime Fresh

Delectable recipes for preparing,
preserving, and celebrating local produce

Elisabeth Bailey

**Photography by
Kelly Neil**

NIMBUS
PUBLISHING

Nimbus Publishing Limited
3731 Mackintosh St, Halifax, NS B3K 5A5
(902) 455-4286
nimbus.ca

Printed and bound in China

Author photos: Nancy McCarthy (Elisabeth Bailey),
Michael Tompkins (Kelly Neil) miketompkins.net
Cover & Interior design: Peggy & Co. Design

All photos by Kelly Neil except for photos on pages 34, 58, 96, and 210 courtesy Damian Lidgard; 170 courtesy Elisabeth Bailey; 11, 47, 53, 79, 84, 91, 124, 129, 134, 146, 153, 164, 174, and 182 from istockphoto.com.

Library and Archives Canada Cataloguing in Publication

Bailey, Elisabeth
Maritime fresh : delectable recipes for preparing, preserving, and celebrating local produce / Elisabeth Bailey ; Kelly Neil, photographer.

Includes index.
Issued also in an electronic format.
ISBN 978-1-77108-008-8

1. Cooking—Maritime Provinces. 2. Cooking, Canadian—Maritime style.
3. Cooking (Vegetables). 4. Cooking (Fruit). 5. Cookbooks. I. Neil, Kelly II. Title.

TX715.6.B325 2013   641.59715   C2012-907387-3

Canadä

NOVA SCOTIA
Communities, Culture and Heritage

Canada Council   Conseil des arts
for the Arts   du Canada

Nimbus Publishing acknowledges the financial support for its publishing activities from the Government of Canada through the Canada Book Fund (CBF) and the Canada Council for the Arts, and from the Province of Nova Scotia through the Department of Communities, Culture and Heritage.

Contents

Acknowledgements

The connections of friends, family, and local food producers were essential in allowing me to write this book. I offer the most heartfelt gratitude for the unfailing support of my husband, John; our son, Charlie; and our extended families.

Alice Burdick and Nilanjana Das sustained me with coffee and love, for which I will be forever in their debt. I am also grateful to Niki Jabbour for her personal and professional support—not to mention her excellent gardening advice!

Many thanks go to Joan Bruneau of Terra Nova Cotta Pottery for her warm encouragement and generous loan of dishware for photo shoots.

Farmers and producers who helped me include Peter Hardy of Ashwood Ridge Farm Estate Ltd., Aaron Hiltz of CaananLand Pastured Products, Orrin and Tracy Murdoch of Mirella Rose Farm, Meredith Bell of Ma Bell's Condiments, Svenja Dee of Tulipwood, Incorporated; Chris and Melissa Velden of Flying Apron Cookery; and all the other fine folk at the Lunenburg Farmers' Market and the Mahone Bay Farmers' Market.

Last but far from least, I am grateful to my photographer, Kelly Neil, and my editor, Whitney Moran, for their talent and unfailing dedication, as well as Patrick Murphy and everyone else at Nimbus Publishing. Thank you all!

Introduction

I love local produce. Not just the idea of it; I have a full-bodied passion for the crunch of the apple, the spray of raspberry juice against my tongue as it explodes, the warm, dribbling juice of the tomato, and the tender sweetness of the fresh pea. Each of these is an experience that distills the goodness of life into a single moment, delighting my heart as it nourishes my body.

Beyond just the eating, though, I get great satisfaction from connecting with the source of my food. This can be as simple as a quick, friendly transaction at the farmers' market, or spending a cloudy afternoon gathering berries at a U-pick. The very best moments, however, occur when I work in my own garden. There's no better way to understand food as a living substance than to grow it, and it is for this reason that I warmly recommend you try your hand at growing a little something, even if a full-blown garden isn't in the cards. Basil in a pot on a sunny windowsill will do the trick quite nicely.

As a town-dweller with only moderate gardening ambitions, I still buy, rather than grow, most of the food that my family consumes. I know that when I purchase food I am voting with my dollars for what kind of world we live in. I choose to vote for one that supports friends and neighbours, strengthens the local economy, and is healthiest for my family. I also vote for a world in which farmers wear overalls and feel the sun on their faces, rather than one where "farmer" means an affiliate of a chemical-producing corporation, clad in a rubber suit to protect his or her skin and lungs from the toxins being sprayed on nutrition-poor grocery store produce. I'm guessing you're with me on this one.

That said, the choice to eat local, seasonal food goes far deeper than growing herbs in a pot and changing where you shop. Nothing less than a complete shift around how you cook and store food is needed, and that's easier said than done. When I first began gardening, I would marvel at my bounty—and then, more often than not, waste it because I was not in the habit of using what I had. After a lifetime of shopping at the grocery store—a big, windowless box where seasons do not exist—I was caught in an entrenched pattern of corporate food consumption. With very few exceptions, one can get anything, any time, and the system encourages you to buy what you need for an evening (or, gosh, if you think ahead, an entire week) at a time. I would often come home, sock my produce away in the fridge, and then eat it, cook it, or forget about it within a matter of days. If I accidentally wasted my purchases or under-bought, I went back to the store for more.

Nature doesn't work like that. As any gardener or farmer can tell you, nature's food cycles vacillate between feast and famine. Food appears in a trickle until suddenly there's a deluge. Supporting local farmers means buying their food when they have it, which has only modest overlap with when you might want to eat it. So what do you do when that deluge comes?

Well, you have a few choices. Using your produce wisely means changing your habits and ways of approaching food in the kitchen. The first step is to orient your menu around what you have, rather than what you might buy at the store. To that end, this book is chock full of recipes to turn mountains of just-picked produce into Dinner Tonight. For preservation methods, I focus on freezing and dehydration—what I consider to be the easiest and safest long-term storage methods. I won't tell you how to ferment or can because even though I've experimented with both, I'm strictly an amateur and am in no position to be giving food safety advice about methods that include sterilization concerns. I'll leave that one to the experts—like author Elizabeth Peirce, who does an excellent job describing the ins and outs of canning and fermentation in her food preservation guide, *You Can Too! Canning, Pickling, and Preserving the Maritime Harvest* (Nimbus 2013).

Maritime Fresh focuses on produce for a reason. Traditionally, people in the Maritimes (and indeed all members of the human species) have eaten a far more plant-heavy diet than most of us do today. Eating produce is an essential part of eating what's available, and it's no coincidence that what's available is nearly ideal in terms of providing nutrition and supporting our health. Our farms and our bodies will thank us for moving back in this direction. Therefore, while this book does include several meaty entrées, it leans more toward small, vegetable-focused dishes. I encourage you to consider that vegetable-based meals need not be just for vegetarians, and there's no rule against mixing it up—if you're used to eating meat at every meal, experiment with having a vegetarian dinner every third night and, if it suits you, increasing the number from there. Include

meals that use meat as a flavouring, rather than as the central ingredient.

I often find that people skimp on the vegetable dishes in their nightly cooking because their time and energy to cook is limited, and most of it goes into a meat-based entrée. One way to accommodate a more plant-based diet is to make a generous amount of a vegetable side dish on a daily basis instead of an entrée. Each day, enjoy a fresh vegetable dish and one or two leftovers, creating a constant rotation of fruits and vegetables in your diet with more variety, better nutrition, and either the same or less cooking time and effort as traditional meal-making.

This book is designed to help you cook with what you have, rather than purchase what you cook. It is organized alphabetically by produce type. Keep the "assorted produce" recipes in mind for days when you have a bit of everything or wish to use up assorted frozen or dried produce. Once you have gained a little experience with the basic tools and methods common to these recipes, you'll find that you are more at liberty to garden food plants without wastage, take advantage of unexpected bounty and good deals at the farmers' market, and make strong use of a Community-Supported Agriculture program. (For more about CSAs, *see* page 230.)

When we make dinner, we're also making meaning—for ourselves and for our families. The more connected we are to the life cycle of our food, the more connected we are, period. How we approach our food has just about everything to do with how we live our lives, so I invite you to fill your plate with the most vibrant and mindfully sourced produce you can get your hands on...and find joy in every bite!

Gathering Your Produce

There are many retailers for local, in-season produce around the Maritimes. Farm markets, small, local retailers, farmers' markets, CSAs, and U-picks are all valuable sources for connecting with local produce. But the freshest and most local produce, of course, comes from your backyard.

Growing and Harvesting Your Own Garden

Whether you're an experienced food gardener or just contemplating the possibility, there's no activity like growing some of your own produce to deepen your relationship with the cycle of life and your place within it. There's a vast body of knowledge and advice about how best to do this, but if you're looking for a starting place I recommend *Grow Organic* also by Elizabeth Peirce (Nimbus 2010)—it's an invaluable guide to the growing conditions and patterns in the Maritimes and how to produce clean, high-quality fruits and vegetables that you can be proud of.

Once you have some gardening experience, I encourage you to expand your growing operations—not necessarily in terms of size, but season. Using inexpensive cold frames and row cover, you can extend your growing year to provide your household with fresh, hearty greens and root vegetables throughout the winter. Storing fresh food in the ground is even easier than keeping it in the pantry or root cellar.

Lastly, I have found that timing your harvest is essential to successful food use and preservation. It's best to harvest at the peak of taste. One of the best things you can do for yourself as a kitchen gardener is let your garden teach you when the produce is ripe to pluck. You'll find that it's usually better to harvest a tad earlier than later. Developing a feel for when that tomato, squash, or cucumber is perfect for eating is part of being connected to your food. That said, it's better to harvest on the day you have time to cook, dry, freeze, or otherwise process your produce than to harvest it when the food is ready but you are not. If that means letting things ride until the weekend, so be it.

Shopping the Farmers' Market

The farmers' market is where thousands of Maritimers connect with local produce, and it's certainly one of my favourite community get-togethers. Shopping at the farmers' market is a lot more interactive than shopping at the grocery store, and it's also more rewarding in just about every way.

If you're a rookie farmers' market shopper, here

USE WHAT?

For the season-extension newbies, a **cold frame** is a box frame, most often constructed of wood, on top of soil, with a clear plastic or glass top. Plants grow inside, benefiting from the light insulation and wind protection the frame provides. **Row cover** is a sheet of transparent (or semitransparent) material, usually plastic, that covers a row or section of growing garden plants. It is often tacked down over wire hooping to form a tunnel. Row cover laid lightly and directly over plants is called **floating row cover**.

is my best piece of advice: go early. My apologies if you're not a morning person, but it really is the best time by far. Be there a few minutes before they open so you can walk around and get the lay of the land (but do not attempt to start buying before the official start time, please—it's disrespectful to the both the farmers and the other customers). In my experience, some of the most exciting, unusual, and delicious items come to the market in small amounts and, if the market begins at 8:00, they are gone by 8:10, the farmer will have filled in the spaces they occupied on their tables, and you'll never even know what you missed.

It's also a good idea to arrive with a plan, albeit one with some wiggle room. I keep two shopping lists—one for the grocery store and one for the farmers' market. Over time I've seen the former get shorter and the latter longer, as I organize my week around going to the market first and then the grocery store later that day or the next. This way, I can shop the market first and fill in any holes at the grocery store instead of the other way around.

Shopping at the farmers' market can be expensive—it's often laden with high-quality, handmade goods and luxurious baby vegetables—but it can also be a place to economize. Buy in season and in volume. Get to know the farmers, then ask if they have any ugly or bruised produce that you can buy at a discount. Process any damaged produce the same day. I've paid less than half of the regular price for tomatoes too ugly for display, but the taste of the sauce I made with them wasn't any less exquisite. Gorgeous baby vegetables are tempting the first week you see them at the market, but they're also pricey. Get just a little taste if you can't resist, but save major buying until they're at the height of their season. If you don't know when that is, ask the farmer! He or she will probably be glad to tell you when the farm is likely to have so much on hand that it's difficult to move it all, and will appreciate meeting someone interested in buying generously when the price is lowest. It is often possible to get an additional price break if you buy a flat or bushel at a time. For the best deals and highest-quality produce, ask the farmers what they recommend. While you're at it, ask them how they like to prepare it at home. Nobody can give you better insight into a fruit or vegetable than the person who grew it, and most of them are experts at quick, easy preparations that bring out the best flavour.

You'll want to bring several things with you to the market. To begin with, bring small bills, loonies, and toonies; it's considerate to the vendors and will win you their favour. I admit to being a little gleeful whenever I hand a fifty-dollar bill to the convenience store clerk to buy a pack of gum, because I'm getting so much change for the market. Also bring good shopping bags or a basket—a sturdy backpack works well if you'll be walking around for a while. To that end, wear comfortable shoes. Lastly, be sure to bring both your manners and your patience. As much as I enjoy chitty-chatting with vendors at the market, it can be a drag to stand in line after line while the people in front of you catch up on personal news with the sellers. I can tell you from experience that it's especially aggravating when you're shopping with a fussy baby or toddler! Nevertheless, some people will neither step up the pace nor miss their chance to chew the fat, so come prepared to accept the way it is and, if you have children with you, bring a surprise toy or activity to pass the time. That said, just because other people don't give a thought to the schedules of the folks in line behind them doesn't mean you shouldn't. Whether it's busy at the market or not, save your socializing for times when nobody is left waiting.

Community-Supported Agriculture (CSA)

I have been delighted to watch Community-Supported Agriculture (CSA) programs growing in leaps and bounds in the Maritimes over the past few years. CSA is an arrangement in which a customer buys a share of a food producer's yield during a growing season or a year. Most often this takes the form of a weekly box of food that the customer picks up either at the farm or at a drop-off site. It's a valuable tool for consumers, who usually save money overall and get the convenience of a diversity of produce at once, and also develop a meaningful relationship with the person who grows their food. For the producer, it provides a predictable and consistent stream of income that can make the difference

in whether or not a farm stays afloat. In many CSAs, the consumer can work on the farm as partial payment for their share. Some people find this a highly rewarding experience—not only does it offer great gardening experience and a personal connection with their source of food, but it's a wellspring of social connection as well. CSA participants and their farmers get to know one another as they share the risk in bad growing seasons, and share the bounty in good ones.

Most CSAs offer produce, and several also offer meat, eggs, and other farm products. CSAs are all different, and the one your friend belongs to may or may not be a good fit for you. Before signing up, ask some of the following questions:

Season Length

On what dates does the CSA operate? Is it year-round, nine months, or summer and fall only? If the CSA does extend past the traditional growing season, what kinds of items are packed in winter boxes?

Size

How big is a share? Of course this depends on weather and a host of other factors at any given time, but what's the average? The most common answer is about enough for a family of four for a week. You may wish to purchase a large amount and do some of your own preservation, or you may prefer a smaller share or half-share.

Offerings

What crops does the farm usually grow? We all prefer some fruits and vegetables to others, so look for a CSA that offers your personal favourites.

Farm Practices

What growing methods are used at the farm? Sustainable farming methods generally produce healthier crops, and organic foods produce a healthier you! In addition to food, a well-run farm can be a rich source of education for CSA participants about how ecosystems work. Depending on your relationship with the farmer, you may or may not care about organic certification.

Distribution System

How will you receive your shares? What is the back-up procedure if you miss a pick-up or go on vacation? Some CSAs require you to visit the farm, some arrange drop-offs at central locations at prearranged times, and some will deliver to your doorstep. Choose an option that will work for you and your schedule.

Payment System

What is the payment schedule? Some CSAs want half or all of a season's payment in advance, while others will allow you to pay quarterly or even monthly. There may or may not be an initial fee.

Flexibility

Is it an option to purchase more on occasion? If you are hosting company or putting up a whompload of tomato sauce for winter, you may wish to make a bulk purchase of some kind from your CSA partner. Some farms are happy to fill extra orders, but others simply don't operate that way.

The number of CSAs in the Maritimes and what they have to offer changes every year. Luckily, Atlantic Canadian Organic Regional Network (ACORN) keeps an excellent, up-to-date database online (*see* Appendix B, page 230).

U-picks

The hands-down most affordable way to purchase bulk produce is by visiting a U-pick and harvesting your own. (Links for finding U-picks in your area can be found in Appendix B.) Here are some tips for making your U-pick experience pleasant, and one you'll want to repeat:

Make a Plan

If you're visiting a U-pick for a fun experience and some fresh food, you may wish to be careful not to pick too much. You don't want to waste money or food. If, however, you plan to freeze, dehydrate, or otherwise preserve the produce you pick, think through about how much you'd like to bring home before you go. Bring containers appropriate for transporting produce back to your home and, if necessary, coolers and ice packs.

Dress for Work, Not Play

You want to be comfortable while you pick, so choose sturdy shoes and light but long-sleeved shirts and light pants. I also recommend hats with brims, for shade, and sunscreen. It's a good idea to bring insect repellent with you, but wait to see whether it's needed or not before applying it—no sense in putting chemicals on your skin if the bugs aren't bothering you.

Make Personal Contact

The farmer or farm employee at the U-pick is an expert; he or she can tell you how to identify produce at the height of ripeness, educate you about different varietals available, and point you toward the best areas for picking.

MYSTERY PRODUCE

Sometimes while you're shopping at the farmers' market you'll see something gorgeous and fresh and buy it on a whim, and later realize that you don't actually know quite what it is. If you belong to a CSA, you may have a similar experience with a fruit or vegetable that appears in your weekly box. You know it's edible...just not what it is or how to eat it! A caveat: unless a mystery fruit or vegetable is sold to you as food by a knowledgeable food producer, do *not* take any chances. Some of the most gorgeous berries and enticing greens you'll find in the woods are poisonous. If you are sure, however, that something is edible, here are some tips for how to cook that which you cannot name:

- Root vegetables can be peeled, chopped, and roasted. Combine 1 pound of bite-sized chunks of any root vegetable with 1 tablespoon extra-virgin olive oil, and add salt, pepper, and any other desired spices to taste. Roast at 400°F until tender, about 45–60 minutes.

- Tender greens can be tossed in a salad (*see* Making Your Own Vinaigrette, page 129).

- Hearty greens can be braised. First pan-fry a bit of diced onion, garlic, or leek in butter or olive oil over medium heat, then add chopped greens, stir, and add about a ½ cup of stock or wine. Cover, reduce heat to low, and simmer mixture until tender.

- Other mystery vegetables can be popped into the stockpot. When in doubt, make a soup. (That's good advice for life, actually.) Pretty much any vegetable or combination of vegetables can be cut into bite-sized pieces, sautéed with butter or oil for a few minutes, tossed in a pot of vegetable or chicken stock, cooked until tender, and enjoyed. Add rice or potatoes to make a stew. Puree and add cream to make a bisque. Keep in mind that any soup or stew likes a bit of chopped, fresh herb on top.

Finally, whatever it is you're eating, even if you don't know...enjoy it!

Have Fun!

It should go without saying, but if you don't enjoy your experience, you won't be likely to repeat it. Make a day of it if you can afford the time. Many U-picks feature attractions such as corn mazes, playgrounds, and petting zoos, so by all means take the kids (and something else for them to do when they inevitably get tired of picking and you're still filling baskets)!

Preserving Your Produce

Even if you do not purposely grow or buy more produce than you plan to use fresh, it's inevitable that you will end up with some extras from time to time that you don't want to let go to waste. Whether for efficiency, supporting local growers, or expanding your garden, it's an excellent idea to

try your hand at preserving produce and making yourself at least a few treats for winter. It's easier than you think, and you'll be surprised at just how much you can save for a snowy day, even if you don't have a chest freezer.

About Freezing

Freezing is my favourite way to preserve produce, and it's often the easiest. Here are some basic principles for freezing produce that will guarantee happy and delicious results.

Leave a Little Room

All food will expand when frozen, so when packing foods to freeze, leave space to accommodate this expansion. I most often freeze food in glass canning jars, which have many advantages—but durability isn't one of them. Trust me, it isn't fun to clean up frozen glass, nor to watch something delicious you worked to create go to waste. That said, if you break a glass food container, *do* let the food go to waste. It's never worth risking the chance that there's a sliver of glass in your food!

Get Liquid With It

It's always better to freeze something wet than something dry, and some fruits should be immersed in syrup before being frozen, in order to preserve them without degradation. To make a simple syrup, combine 2 cups sugar and 4 cups water in a saucepan, and bring just to a boil over medium heat. Remove from heat, cool, and pour over packed chunks of fruit. I normally use white sugar to make a simple syrup, but you can also use raw sugar, brown sugar, or honey to taste.

RHUBARB EXTRACT

Although I'm not a complete purist when it comes to eating locally, I always have an eye out for local alternatives to standard ingredients in my recipes. I'm not a huge fan of vinegar, so when recipes call for acid I tend toward lemon juice instead. One day, however, I looked out my kitchen window at a clump of rhubarb and said to myself, "Hold the phone...those are chock full of acid. How do I get it out?"

Use this potent liquid as an alternative to lemon juice in many recipes, or to make a delightful rhubarbade with the addition of sugar and either flat or sparkling water. Rhubarb, although very acidic, isn't quite as acidic as lemon juice, so keep that in mind when making substitutions. Most lemon juice has a pH of around 2.1. I measured the acidity of my rhubarb extract at 2.9 (yes, I'm one of those geeks who keeps a pH meter lying around). That's not quite as close as it sounds because pH is measured logarithmically, like earthquakes. It is, nonetheless, acidic enough to achieve the desired effect in many recipes. If you use lemon juice to add acidity for pickling, be aware that you want the overall acidity to be a pH of 4.3 or under, so rhubarb extract can sometimes be used effectively used for that purpose.

To prepare: Cook 4 cups chopped rhubarb over medium-low heat, covered, stirring occasionally, until fibres have completely broken down into the liquid. Set aside to cool for 20 minutes, then strain through a colander lined with cheesecloth. Squeeze cheesecloth firmly to extract all liquid. Transfer rhubarb to ice cube trays and freeze. Once frozen, seal in a freezer bag until ready for use.

> **pH** measures how acidic (like lemon juice) or basic (like Milk of Magnesia) something is on a scale of 0 to 14. Seven is neutral; values above that are basic and those below are acidic. A little acid in food adds flavour, and a lot keeps it from spoiling, because bacteria can't live in a highly acidic environment. That's why canners are especially concerned with acidity—they want to make sure their canned goods don't go bad on the shelf!

Blanch as Directed

You will notice that my notes on freezing vegetables usually include an instruction to blanch. Blanching is the process of scalding vegetables in boiling hot water without actually cooking them. Depending on the size and density of the vegetable, this usually takes between 1 to 5 minutes. It can seem like an irritating extra step, but it's a necessary one, and here's why: good, real, fresh produce is alive. It's full of enzymes, which continue to do their work of growing and maturing the vegetables after they've been harvested, and even after they're frozen. While this enzymatic action is a testament to the quality of fresh produce, it can negatively affect the taste of frozen foods. Blanching arrests enzymatic action and prepares vegetables to be frozen, preserving their flavour and nutrition. Although it *is* possible to blanch vegetables by steaming them, consistency is easier to achieve by boiling.

Boil 4 litres of water for every pound of vegetables, then gently lower vegetables into water in a metal colander or steaming basket, and blanch for the recommended time. When the time is up, remove vegetables and immediately plunge into a bowl or pot of ice water for a couple of minutes to keep them from over-blanching or cooking. Drain and freeze according to instruction.

About Drying

Dehydration removes water from food. Without water, bacteria and mould can't grow. Dehydrated foods keep even longer than frozen ones, and take up far less space. Despite my persistent dreams of laying out racks of Italian-style sun-dried tomatoes (I'm always wearing a dirndl in these fantasies), the Maritimes simply don't get hot and dry enough for safe sun-drying to be a possibility. Therefore, although I normally eschew specialty equipment, there's one gadget I strongly recommend to home cooks: a food dehydrator.

For about seventy dollars, a food dehydrator will vastly extend your ability to preserve food throughout the growing season. Although most foods I put in my dehydrator can also be dried in the oven, the dehydrator does a far better job with less energy, and doesn't contribute heat to the house on a warm summer day the way an oven can. If you don't have the equipment but are itching to get started, here's how: set the temperature of your oven to 180°F and prop the door open slightly. This method will help you get the inside of the oven to the temperature you actually want, between 120°F and 140°F. (Note: this is not safe to do with curious pets or children around, which is another good reason to invest in a dehydrator.)

Dry both fruits and vegetables, sliced and arranged on the drying trays in a single layer, with a bit of space between pieces. Vegetables should be dried at 130°F and fruits at 135°F. Drying times can vary widely, depending on the initial moisture of the produce, the size of the pieces dried, and the particularities of your dehydrator. Test to see if food is dried enough by tearing a piece open and looking for beads of moisture. If the outside is leathery to the touch and there is no visible moisture, it's done. If you continue to dry past this point until food is brittle, it will still keep and taste good, but it will lose some of its nutritive value, so I don't recommend it.

Should you blanch before dehydrating vegetables as well? Some sources say yes. In my experience, the removal of moisture seems to be sufficient to keep enzymatic action from affecting the taste or quality of dried produce, so I generally don't bother, but if you're the meticulous sort you may wish to add this extra step.

If you're particularly concerned about the colour of your dried fruit, you may soak fruit in a lemon- or rhubarb-juice solution for a couple of minutes before arranging it on the dryer racks. (You may wish to do this especially for apples, pears, and peaches.) In these cases, make an acidic solution of 1 tablespoon lemon juice or 2 tablespoons rhubarb juice to 2 cups water. Store dried food in an airtight jar or plastic freezer bag. Food stays in good shape even longer if you suck the excess air out of the bag with a straw. I store most of my dried produce in the freezer anyway, just to be on the safe side.

Many dried fruits make great snacks and ingredients in their dried state. In some cases, such as with strawberries, I find that the dehydrated version is even more appetizing than the fresh for eating out of hand because the sugars are concentrated, making for a sweeter, more flavourful snack. For cooking and baking purposes, however, you will want to rehydrate many fruits, and nearly all vegetables. To do this, simply immerse the dried produce in liquid for 1 to 2 hours until the hydration level appears to be similar to fresh produce. For faster rehydration,

use liquid that has been brought to a simmer then removed from heat just before adding the produce.

Since the dehydration process removes water you can, of course, use water to rehydrate, but I usually use another liquid instead, in order to layer and intensify the flavours in a dish. For fruit, I use a juice that complements the flavour of the fruit, such as local apple cider, blueberry juice, or white grape juice. For vegetables, I use vegetable or chicken stock or, occasionally, wine. You can even use milk or coconut milk to rehydrate produce that you plan to use in a creamy dish. The people who eat your cooking will never guess what you did to make it so delicious—they'll just admire your prowess in the kitchen!

Apples

pples are one of the most diverse and healthful fruits in the human diet, and my personal favourite. They've also been a major player in Maritime agricultural history since the days of the Acadians, and several unique varietals, such as Nova Spy and Nova Mac, have been developed at local agricultural research stations.

Apples can be kept on a cool counter for up to 2 weeks, depending upon the varietal. Many apples can be stored for longer in the refrigerator, but it's generally a better idea to use them within 1 week or so. Of course, most apples are excellent eaten out of hand. I like to keep apples in a bowl of salted water, treated liberally with lemon juice, on hot summer days.

To freeze apples: peel, core, quarter, combine with simple syrup (*see* Get Liquid With It, page 8) to cover in a saucepan, bring almost to a simmer over medium heat, remove from heat, add 1 teaspoon of lemon or rhubarb juice, pack, and freeze.

To dehydrate apples: peel, core, slice, and dry at 135°F for 6 to 12 hours.

Other recipes using apples include Plum Applesauce (*see* page 172) and Berry Maritime Rumtopf (226).

Apple Butter

**Yield: approximately
4 pints**

- -

10 medium apples,
   peels on, cored
   and sliced
2 cups unsweetened
   apple juice
¼ cup water
¼ cup apple cider
   vinegar
1 tablespoon
   cinnamon
½ teaspoon vanilla
¼ teaspoon ground
   cloves
¼ teaspoon ground
   nutmeg
Pinch salt

This apple butter recipe comes from Tracy Murdoch of Mirella Rose Farm in Lunenburg County, Nova Scotia, which offers a unique "whole diet" CSA (*see page 17*).

Apple butter is a great condiment for pork, and is a family favourite for morning toast and pancakes. Somewhat similar to applesauce, apple butter is less sweet and better suited to dressing meats. Keeping the peels on adds a welcome texture, flavour, and nutritional boost to the finished butter. Typically keeps for 1 week in the refrigerator, or 6 months in the freezer.

Combine all ingredients in a stockpot. Cover and cook on low heat, stirring occasionally, until apples break down, about 3 hours. Remove from heat and allow to cool for 30 minutes.

Puree with an immersion blender, or transfer to a stand blender and puree. Transfer finished apple butter to sealed containers, and store in the refrigerator or freezer.

Maple Apple Pork

Serves 4

- -

1 pound boneless
   pork tenderloin,
   cut into bite-sized
   pieces
2 teaspoons Herb
   Salt (*see* page 120),
   or 1 teaspoon plain
   salt
½ teaspoon pepper
2 tablespoons butter
1 onion, finely
   chopped
3 large apples,
   peeled, cored, and
   chopped (fresh,
   rehydrated, dried,
   or frozen)
2 tablespoons maple
   syrup
¼ cup Vegetable
   Stock
   (*see* page 224)
¼ cup minced fresh
   parsley (optional)

Apples, maple syrup, and pork—a classic combination, and for excellent reason (as your taste buds will attest).

Rub pork tenderloin with salt and pepper. Heat a sauté pan on medium heat, then add butter and pork. Sauté until browned (2–3 minutes).

Remove pork from pan and add onion. Continue to sauté, stirring frequently, for 5 minutes. Add apples and sauté another 5 minutes.

Return pork to the pan, and add maple syrup and stock. Reduce heat to low, cover, and simmer until pork is cooked through, about 5 minutes. Garnish with parsley (if desired) and serve with pasta or rice.

MACINTOSH
$5.00

Tonagou

Upside-Down Apple Walnut Cake

Serves 8

----

3 cups peeled,
    cored, and finely
    chopped apples
    (any varietal)
1 cup butter, divided
⅔ cup brown sugar,
    lightly packed
1 cup coarsely
    chopped walnuts
1½ cups all-purpose
    flour
1½ teaspoons baking
    powder
½ cup white sugar
1 teaspoon cinnamon
½ teaspoon salt
1 teaspoon allspice
2 teaspoons vanilla
2 large eggs
¾ cup plain, full-fat
    yogurt

Unless you're using Cortlands (which don't brown), keep your apples in a bowl of water dosed with lemon or rhubarb juice to keep them fresh while you peel and chop.

Preheat oven to 375°F.

Combine ½ cup of the butter, chopped apples, brown sugar, and walnuts in a cast iron pan and sauté over low heat, stirring frequently, until apples are cooked and sugar is caramelized, about 30 minutes.

In the meantime, combine flour, baking powder, white sugar, cinnamon, salt, and allspice in a mixing bowl and whisk together.

In a second mixing bowl, combine other ½ cup of butter, vanilla, eggs, and yogurt and cream together well. Add dry ingredients to the mixture and stir until an even batter forms.

Pour batter over the apple and walnut mixture in the cast iron pan, and transfer the pan to the oven. Bake until cake is golden-brown and a knife inserted in the middle comes out clean, about 30 minutes. Cool on a rack, then serve.

Apple Raisin Chutney

**Yield: approximately
1 quart**

- -

4 large or 7 small
  apples (any varietal
  or combination),
  peeled, cored, and
  chopped
1 cup lemon juice
1 cup packed brown
  sugar
1 onion, minced
½ tablespoon red
  pepper flakes
2 tablespoons
  minced fresh
  ginger
1 stick cinnamon
1 cup raisins

This is a great condiment for poultry or pork for an easy meal, chock full of homemade flavour, any time of year. Double the amount of red pepper flakes in this recipe if you like your chutney particularly spicy.

Combine all ingredients in a saucepan and bring to a simmer over medium-low heat. Continue to simmer, stirring occasionally, for 1 hour. Discard cinnamon stick. Serve warm or cold. Chutney keeps in the refrigerator for 1 week, or the freezer for 6 months.

MIRELLA ROSE FARM

Mirella Rose Farm, just outside of Mahone Bay, Nova Scotia, offers a unique "whole-diet" CSA. Rather than package a particular amount of food, farmers Tracy and Orrin Murdoch encourage participants to take as much as they need to meet their household needs. Foods offered include beef, pork, chicken, eggs, and a wide variety of fresh and storage produce, including year-round salad greens. Participants are even welcome to a share of the wool shorn from the farm's Shetland sheep.

To join the Mirella Rose CSA, each member of a household must be a member. Shares for children aged three to thirteen are half-price, and children under three are included in their parents' shares. Members must also commit for a whole calendar year. This model of CSA is considered to be both high investment and high return, and is a terrific way for someone who wishes to eat an extremely fresh, nutritious, and entirely local diet to do so without farming themselves.

To learn more, phone Tracy and Orrin Murdoch at 902-623-0045 or email them at tracy@organic-matters.ca.

Baked Breakfast Apples

Serves 4

----

4 large apples (any
   varietal)
1½ cups granola
1 cup cream cheese
½ cup milk

This quick and easy breakfast beats the pants off of boxed cereal. If you're crafty, carve out a face from the apple top and replace it over the baked apple before serving—your family will feel the love all day long.

Preheat oven to 350°F and generously butter a baking dish.

Using a small, sharp knife, remove the core of each apple while leaving the rest of the apple whole. Place apples in prepared baking dish.

Combine granola, cream cheese, and milk in a mixing bowl. Spoon mixture into apples. Bake for 1 hour. Serve hot or at room temperature.

Cheddar Apple Pie

Serves 8

- -

2¼ cups pastry flour
(all-purpose will
do in a pinch)
1 cup shredded
cheddar cheese
1 cup cold butter, cut
into small pieces
½ cup cold milk
3 pounds apples
(any varietal or a
mixture), peeled,
cored, and
chopped into
bite-sized pieces
⅔ cup sugar
1 tablespoon
cornstarch
1 tablespoon lemon
juice
½ teaspoon ground
nutmeg
¼ teaspoon salt

You may also use pears or a combination of apples and pears (or, for that matter, plums) in this recipe. If you're not terrific at rolling out and shaping pie crust—it's certainly not my strong point—feel free to press torn pieces together for both the bottom and top crusts. It won't be quite as pretty but it will taste just as fabulous, I promise. Don't let fear of a tricky technique keep you from enjoying your kitchen adventures in this or any other recipe. If, on the other hand, you're very clever and crafty with dough, you can cut out shapes from the top crust with a small cookie cutter to make steam vents instead of cutting slits, or you can cut the top crust into strips and weave a lattice. Have fun with it!

Combine flour, cheddar, butter, and milk in a mixing bowl or food processor. Cut together until dough just holds together. Wrap ball of dough in plastic wrap and reserve in refrigerator for at least 2 hours, or overnight.

Preheat oven to 450°F. In a mixing bowl combine chopped apples, sugar, cornstarch, lemon juice, nutmeg, and salt. Stir until apples are thoroughly coated.

Remove dough from refrigerator. Divide into 2 parts and roll into 2 large rounds. Arrange one in the bottom of a 9-inch pie plate.

Transfer filling on top of bottom crust, then gently transfer larger crust to the top, and seal edges to top of bottom crust. Cut several slits in the top crust to vent steam.

Bake for 20 minutes, then reduce heat to 375°F and bake until crust is browned and filling is bubbling-hot, about another 40 minutes. Cool on a rack and serve warm or cool.

Asparagus

Asparagus has been cultivated for thousands of years in Egypt, India, and the Himalayas. As one of the first vegetables of spring and a superior candidate for preserving, it has long held an important role in the Maritime diet.

Choose or harvest thin, firm stems with closed tips. If allowed to grow too fat, asparagus will become tough and woody. If you won't be using it right away, keep asparagus upright in a vase or bowl with 1 to 2 inches of water at the bottom. It does not need to be refrigerated. Use within 4 to 5 days. Cooked asparagus is delicious cold as well as hot—try it tossed with pasta and herbs for a particularly easy meal.

To freeze, trim asparagus spears, blanch thin spears for 2 minutes or thick ones for 4, and pack in a plastic freezer bag with as much air as possible removed. I do not recommend dehydrating asparagus.

You may also pickle asparagus, substituting asparagus spears for carrots in Spicy Lemon Carrot Pickles (*see* page 66).

Asparagus Tofu Curry

Serves 4

- -

3 tablespoons
   sesame oil
1 onion, minced
1 pound firm tofu,
   diced into cubes
3 cups fresh
   asparagus, diced
2 teaspoons red
   curry paste
1 cup plain,
   full-fat yogurt
Minced basil to
   taste, up to
   5 tablespoons

This lively dish is simply fabulous for showcasing fresh asparagus in a company dinner.

Heat sesame oil in a sauté pan over medium-high heat. Add minced onion and tofu cubes and sauté, stirring frequently, until onion and tofu are both browned and onion is soft (8–10 minutes).

Turn heat down to medium. Add asparagus and continue to cook, stirring frequently, for 4 minutes, or until asparagus is cooked but still bright green and firm.

Turn heat to low and add curry paste, yogurt, and basil, and stir to combine. Heat until warmed through. Serve with white or brown rice.

Cream of Asparagus Soup

Serves 4

----

4 tablespoons butter

1 onion, minced

2 teaspoons Herb
   Salt (*see* page 120)
   or 1 teaspoon plain
   salt

2 cups Vegetable
   Stock (*see* page
   224) or chicken
   stock

1 pound asparagus,
   cleaned and diced
   (fresh, frozen
   and thawed, or
   dehydrated and
   rehydrated)

2 tablespoons flour

1 clove garlic, minced

¼ cup grated
   Parmesan

1½ cups light (10%)
   cream (or ½ cup
   heavy [35%] cream
   and 1 cup whole
   milk)

This is an excellent soup for freezing. Simply ladle into containers and freeze before adding the cream and Parmesan, then defrost and continue the recipe any time of year. I love this soup as a warm-me-up on snowy days.

Combine the butter, onion, and salt in a stockpot and sauté on medium-low heat, stirring occasionally, until onion is soft, about 10 minutes.

Add stock and asparagus, and simmer until asparagus is tender and cooked through, about 10 minutes.

Puree with a stick blender or remove to a stand blender, puree, and return to the pot.

Return to heat and sprinkle in flour while stirring. Add garlic, Parmesan, and cream, and simmer on medium-low for 15 minutes. Serve hot.

Asparagus Bread Pudding

Serves 8

- -

2 tablespoons butter

1 onion, minced

1 teaspoon dry
   mustard

1 pound asparagus,
   trimmed and
   cut into bite-
   sized pieces
   (fresh, frozen
   and thawed, or
   dehydrated and
   rehydrated)

6 eggs

2 cups full-fat milk

3 teaspoons Herb
   Salt (*see* page 120)
   or 1½ teaspoons
   plain salt

Pepper to taste

2½ cups shredded
   Gouda or cheddar

1 cup grated
   Parmesan

1 loaf bread, cubed
   into bite-sized
   pieces and left out
   to dry for a day

A savoury bread pudding not only makes a satisfying dinner on a cool spring night, but it's also an impressive contribution to a potluck. The quality of the dish depends on the quality of the bread used, so choose a flavourful favourite.

Combine butter, onion, and dry mustard in a sauté pan and sauté on medium-low, stirring occasionally, until onion is soft, about 10 minutes.

Steam asparagus in 1 inch of water until cooked but still firm, about 3 minutes. Drain, rinse with cool water, and set aside.

Preheat oven to 375°F and butter a baking dish.

Combine eggs, milk, salt, and pepper in a mixing bowl and whisk thoroughly. Add cheeses, onion mixture, asparagus, and bread and stir to combine. Transfer mixture to baking dish.

Bake until pudding is completely set and browned on top, about 45 minutes. Allow to cool for 10 minutes, then serve.

Beans

If you've only ever had dried and canned beans, mature beans that you grow yourself or purchase freshly picked will be a gustatory revelation. Green beans should be stored loose in an airtight container with a damp towel in the refrigerator for a few days. Fresh, mature beans should be cooked within the day or dried for future use. Fresh, young green beans need only 1–2 minutes of steaming, until they turn a bright green.

To cook fresh, mature beans, soak for a couple of hours then just barely cover with water in a stockpot. Cook slowly over low heat, uncovered, adding more water only if necessary. Add a pinch of salt at the beginning of the process and another one at the end. Cook until tender (40–60 minutes).

To cook dried beans, follow the same process but with longer soaking and cooking times. Soak dried beans overnight and cook them until tender, about 3 hours.

To freeze green beans, cut into bite-sized pieces, blanch for 3 minutes, pack plain or in stock, and freeze. To dry fresh, mature beans, simply let them dry on the vine in their pods, then pack and store in the pantry or freezer. To dehydrate green beans, cut into bite-sized pieces, blanch, and dry until nearly brittle.

Other recipes calling for beans include Parmesan Cabbage Bean Soup (*see* page 63) and Twice-Baked Potatoes (176). You may also pickle green beans, substituting asparagus spears for carrots in Spicy Lemon Carrot Pickles (66).

Green Bean Casserole

Serve over rice for an entrée, or as a side dish as part of a heavier meal.

2½ cups green
beans, trimmed
and cut into
bite-sized pieces
(fresh, dried
and rehydrated,
or frozen and
thawed)
1 cup Garlic Chicken
Stock (*see* page
107) or Vegetable
Stock (224)
½ cup heavy (35%)
cream
1 tablespoon flour
1 tablespoon butter
2 tablespoons grated
Parmesan
Salt and pepper to
taste
2 tablespoons sliced
almonds

Combine green beans and stock in a saucepan over low heat. Cover and simmer until green beans are tender, about 10 minutes. Add cream, flour, butter, Parmesan, and salt and pepper and simmer for another 5 minutes, stirring frequently. Top with sliced almonds and serve immediately.

Garlic Green Bean Rigatoni

Serves 4

- -

16 ounces (450 g)
   dried rigatoni (or
   other pasta)

3 cups trimmed
   green beans
   (fresh, dried
   and rehydrated,
   or frozen and
   thawed)

3 tablespoons soy
   sauce

3 cloves garlic,
   minced or pressed

2 tablespoons
   toasted sesame oil

1 tablespoon sesame
   seeds

When I'm feeling moderately fancy I make this dish with tricoloured vegetable pasta—when I'm feeling very fancy I make my own.

Bring a large pot of salted water to a boil over medium-high heat. Add rigatoni and boil for 5 minutes, then add green beans. Boil another 2 minutes, or until rigatoni and green beans are both cooked through. Drain and return to pot.

In the meantime, whisk soy sauce, garlic, and sesame oil together. Add mixture to drained pasta and green beans.

Return pot to low heat for 3 minutes, then add sesame seeds, stir to combine, and remove from heat. Serve immediately.

Ginger Bean Potato Salad

Serves 6

This well-rounded salad makes a good, light lunch all by itself.

2 pounds new
   potatoes, cut into
   bite-sized pieces
8 cloves garlic,
   peeled and
   chopped
2 teaspoons Herb
   Salt (see page 120)
   or 1 teaspoon plain
   salt
½ cup extra-virgin
   olive oil, divided
1 pound fresh green
   beans, trimmed
   and chopped
1 tablespoon finely
   grated ginger
1 tablespoon lemon
   juice

Preheat oven to 325°F.

Combine potatoes, garlic, salt, and half the olive oil in a mixing bowl and toss well. Transfer to a baking sheet and roast until potatoes are tender, about 1 hour.

Bring a pot of salted water to a boil over medium-high heat. Add green beans to water and boil until tender but still bright green, about 3 minutes. Drain and rinse with cool water.

Combine remaining ¼ cup of olive oil, ginger, and lemon juice in a mixing bowl and whisk vigorously to form a vinaigrette. Add roasted potatoes, garlic, and cooked green beans; toss well, and serve immediately.

Bean and Roasted Tomato Stew

Serves 4

----

3 pounds tomatoes
  (any varietal),
  sliced

⅓ cup extra-virgin
  olive oil

4 cloves garlic, finely
  chopped

2 teaspoons Herb
  Salt (*see* page 120)
  or 1 teaspoon plain
  salt

3 cups cooked beans
  (any varietal)

3 cups Garlic Chicken
  Stock (*see* page
  107) or Vegetable
  Stock (224)

⅓ cup finely
  chopped fresh
  basil

This dish is an excellent way to showcase the flavourful nature of garden beans and tomatoes, and is also very good with dried and rehydrated versions.

Place an oven rack in the upper-third of the oven; preheat oven to 450°F.

Combine tomatoes, olive oil, garlic, and salt in a shallow baking dish. Roast for 45 minutes.

Combine roasted tomatoes, beans, and stock in a stockpot and heat to a simmer on medium-low. Simmer for 10 minutes, then sprinkle with basil and serve.

Bean and Cheese Burritos

Serves 4 (2 each)

----

1 pound fresh beans
    (any varietal)
2 cloves garlic,
    minced
1 tablespoon cumin
1 teaspoons salt
1 teaspoon black
    pepper
⅓ cup extra-virgin
    olive oil
2 cups grated
    Monterey Jack
1 cup minced green
    onion
1 cup minced cilantro
8 flour tortillas

A burrito doesn't have to be the size of your head and dripping with greasy meat to be deeply satisfying—the rich flavour of fresh beans easily carries this dish.

Bring a large pot of salted water a boil over medium-high heat. Add beans and reduce heat to medium-low. Simmer, stirring occasionally, until beans are tender and cooked through, about 1 hour. Drain beans.

In the meantime, combine garlic, cumin, salt, pepper, and olive oil in a skillet over medium-low heat. Sauté, stirring for 3 minutes, then add cooked beans. Mash in the skillet with a fork or potato masher. Add the grated cheese and continue to cook, stirring until cheese is melted. Remove from heat.

Divide bean mixture between tortillas and top each one with a portion of green onion and cilantro. Fold tortillas over to form a bundle. Serve immediately.

Beets

Beets are one of the very prettiest vegetables—I love the vibrant burgundy of the most common beets, as well as the bull's eye purple-and-white chioggia beet, stripey golden beet, and even the occasional albino beet I find in the baskets at my local farmers' market. And of course, they're all delicious.

If you are growing your own beets, harvest them when they are no greater than two inches across. Larger beets can become dry and woody inside. The sweetest and most tender beets are those from the fall crop that are harvested after the weather turns cool, so plant in the late summer for beets that you wish to preserve or store. You can also cut leaves, here and there, from developing beets to eat as greens.

Beets keep best if you separate the greens from the roots right away. Wash and keep the roots in an open container but covered with a damp towel. The greens, however, should be in an airtight container. Beets will also keep stored in damp sand in a cool place for up to 5 months.

Beets can be boiled, sautéed, or roasted until tender, while beet greens can be cooked like any other hearty green, such as kale or Swiss chard. I do not recommend drying beets. If you wish to freeze them, cook, peel, and slice first.

A word of warning: beets leave a pretty, but stubborn, colour on anything they touch. To get beet colour off your hands, cutting board, or anything else, scrub with baking soda and cold water.

Balsamic Roasted Beets

Serves 6

----

2 pounds red beets,
   peeled and
   chopped into
   bite-sized pieces
¼ cup extra-virgin
   olive oil
¼ cup balsamic
   vinegar
Zest of 1 orange
Salt and pepper to
   taste

This dish is "beety beetville" with a few zesty grace notes for when you just want to beet it up—something I never would have imagined wanting to do before I became a gardener, but now look forward to every year.

Preheat oven to 400°F.

Toss all ingredients in a mixing bowl, then transfer to a large baking dish. Roast beets until they are tender, stirring occasionally, about 1 hour. Serve immediately.

Borscht

**Serves 4 (as a main)
or 8 (as a starter)**

----

8 cups chicken stock
  or Vegetable Stock
  (*see* page 224)
1 onion, finely
  chopped
6 large beets, peeled
  and chopped
4 large carrots,
  peeled and
  chopped
2 cups finely
  chopped cabbage
2 tablespoons lemon
  juice
½ cup minced fresh
  dill or parsley
Salt and pepper to
  taste
1 cup sour cream

A traditional borscht calls for beef shank, but this lighter vegetarian version is all about the fresh produce—especially the beets. Feel free to add up to 1 pound of stew beef with the cabbage if you would like a meaty borscht.

Combine stock, onion, beets, and carrots in a stockpot. Bring to a simmer over medium-low heat and cook until vegetables are crisp-tender, about 30 minutes.

Add cabbage and lemon juice and simmer for another 15 minutes until cabbage is also tender.

Add minced herbs, salt, and pepper. Stir in sour cream and serve immediately.

Spicy Pickled Beets

Yield: about 2 quarts

2½ pounds beets,
    peeled and sliced
    into sticks

6 cloves garlic, finely
    sliced

1 jalapeño, seeded
    and finely
    chopped

2 tablespoons
    minced, fresh
    ginger

¾ cup brown sugar

1 cup lemon juice

1½ cups apple cider
    vinegar

2 teaspoons salt

10 peppercorns

There's a lot of kick to these beets. If you'd like to pickle your own without the heat, just omit the jalapeño. Keep in mind that these pickles are not sterile, so they should be stored in the refrigerator and consumed within 6 weeks.

Combine all ingredients in a stockpot over medium-high heat and bring to a boil. Boil, stirring frequently, for 15 minutes, then transfer mixture to canning jars or other clean containers with tight lids.

Refrigerate for at least 1 week before consuming. Pickled beets will keep in the refrigerator for up to 6 weeks.

Red Wine Beet Risotto

Serves 4

- -

6 tablespoons butter,
    divided
1 onion, minced
2 teaspoons Herb
    Salt (*see* page 120)
    or 1 teaspoon plain
    salt
2 cloves garlic,
    minced or pressed
1 pound beets,
    peeled and diced
1 pound arborio rice
¾ cup red wine
8 cups Garlic
    Chicken Stock
    (*see* page 107) or
    Vegetable Stock
    (224)
1 tablespoon lemon
    juice
1 tablespoon extra-
    virgin olive oil
¾ cup grated
    Parmesan
Pepper to taste

This simple dish makes a wonderful light entrée. If you'd like a little meat to heavy it up, add some crumbled bacon to the top just before serving.

Combine 3 tablespoons of butter, onion, and salt in a sauté pan and sauté on medium-low, stirring occasionally, until onion is soft, about 10 minutes.

Add garlic, beets, and arborio rice, and sauté an additional 2 minutes, stirring. Turn heat to medium; add red wine and cook, stirring, another 2 minutes.

Add stock, one cup at a time, as rice absorbs the liquid, stirring often, until all stock is in the rice, about an hour. Add lemon juice, olive oil, Parmesan, and pepper. Stir to combine and serve immediately.

Berries

All sorts of berries love the acidic soils of the Maritimes. The first thing I planted after moving into my house in Lunenburg nearly a decade ago was a raspberry cane I bought at Canadian Tire. Now the raspberry patch takes up a hefty chunk of the front lawn, despite getting completely mowed down by two separate lawn care companies in the past two years. Strawberries are teaming up with mint and kale to dominate the backyard, and the wild blackberries on the Rails to Trails path a couple of blocks away lure me into picking more than our fill every fall. Each varietal is its own delight.

As anyone who has bought a plastic container of berries at the store can attest, they mould quickly in the fridge, especially raspberries. For years I attributed this to long shipping times and sloppy storage on the part of the store—then I started growing raspberries myself, and I observed that in wet conditions they can mould on the vine as they ripen! They're simply a delicate fruit that requires ideal conditions.

To extend the storage life of your berries, prepare a disinfecting wash of 1 tablespoon white vinegar to ⅔ cup water. Pour mixture over fresh berries to cover, gently swirl, and drain. In many cases, this quick step can nearly double the refrigerator life of your berries.

Aggregate berries, such as blackberries and raspberries, are particularly perishable. Even though they taste best at room temperature, if you aren't going to use them within a couple of hours they should really be refrigerated. They will only keep in the refrigerator for 2 to 3 days untreated, while blueberries and strawberries can be refrigerated for 5 to 6 days. Be especially conscientious to keep strawberries dry.

To freeze berries, pack them in simple syrup (*see* Get Liquid With It, page 8). Aggregate berries should be crushed before freezing (in effect making their own syrup). This can be done with or without added sugar. To dehydrate, slice strawberries but dry other berries whole. All berries should be dried for 12 to 15 hours at 135°F.

Another recipe that uses berries is Berry Maritime Rumtopf (226).

Blackberry Paletas

Serves 8

- -

2½ cups rinsed
blackberries
⅓ cup lemon juice
⅔ cup sugar

This recipe works well for most kinds of berries. It's really just a simple ice pop, and is a great use of fruit that is deliciously ripe today, but will be too ripe tomorrow. When you freeze produce, you capture the height of ripeness in time.

Puree berries in a blender. Force mixture through a fine sieve to remove the seeds. Combine the strained puree with lemon juice and sugar and stir until sugar dissolves.

Pour mixture into a ice pop mould with room for 8. Freeze until firm, about 4 hours.

Alternatively, you can make ice cubes from the mixture. We enjoy these in a glass of sparkling water on a hot summer evening.

Raspberry Milk Liqueur

Yield: 1 quart

- -

2 cups clean, ripe
raspberries,
mashed
2 cups vodka
2 cups (2%) milk
Juice of 1 lemon
Zest of 1 lemon
1 cup sugar

This sweet, fruity liqueur disguises a potent punch. Sip it at a leisurely pace!

Combine all ingredients in a pitcher or mixing bowl. Cover tightly with plastic wrap. Store in a cool, dark place for 10 days, stirring every other day.

Strain mixture through a coffee filter to remove solids. Repeat strain until liquid is a clear, rosy colour. Pour liqueur into a clean bottle. Will keep in the refrigerator for about 4 months.

Berry Agua Fresca

Serves 2

Flesh of 1 small
   or ½ of 1 large
   watermelon, rind
   removed, cut into
   large chunks
1 cup raspberries
   or blueberries
2 teaspoons
   lime juice
2 teaspoons sugar

An *agua fresca* is a traditional Mexican beverage that literally means "fresh water." Less sweet than juice, an *agua fresca* captures the flavour and nutrition of seasonal fruit. It's the perfect refresher between a session of gardening and...another session of gardening!

Mash watermelon chunks and berries by hand with a potato masher or back of a large spoon, and force flesh through a fine sieve to remove seeds. Combine with lime juice and sugar, stir well, and serve.

Sweet and Sour Strawberry Candy

Yield: About 1 cup

6 cups fresh, sliced
   strawberries
½ tablespoon
   citric acid
2 tablespoons sugar,
   or to taste

Certain members of my household think this is the only way to eat strawberries, so be forewarned—it's addictive! You may use coloured sugar to make more vivid candies if you wish. Citric acid is sold in most places that sell specialty baking supplies. I get mine at Bulk Barn.

Combine all ingredients and toss so that pieces are evenly covered with citric acid and sugar. Dehydrate at 135°F until strawberries are dry, about 18 hours.

Berry Cream Cake

Serves 8–10

1⅓ cups all-purpose
flour
2½ teaspoons baking
powder
½ teaspoon salt
1½ cups sugar,
divided
2 large eggs
2 cups heavy (35%)
cream, divided
1 teaspoon almond
extract
3 teaspoons vanilla
extract, divided
2 pounds fresh
berries, washed
and dried (any kind
or a combination;
strawberries
should also be
sliced)

This is a gorgeous company cake—perfect for a summer birthday celebration
or Canada Day picnic.

Preheat oven to 350°F. Generously butter two 9-inch round pans and set
aside. Combine flour, baking powder, and salt in a mixing bowl and whisk
to combine.

In a second mixing bowl, beat 1 cup of the sugar and eggs together,
then add 1 cup of the cream, the teaspoon of almond extract, and
2 teaspoons of the vanilla extract, and beat again.

Add dry ingredients to wet ingredients and stir to combine. Transfer
batter equally to cake pans. Bake for 30 minutes, or until a toothpick
inserted in the centre comes out clean. Cool on a rack.

While cake is cooling, combine berries, remaining ½ cup of sugar,
remaining teaspoon of vanilla extract, and remaining cup of cream in a
mixing bowl and toss.

Spoon half of berry mixture over one cake round, layer second cake
round on top of it, and spoon remaining berry mixture on top. Slice and
serve immediately.

Berry Gelatin

Serves 8

----

1 quart white grape
   juice, divided
4 packets
   unflavoured
   gelatin
1 pound fresh berries
   (any varietal),
   stemmed and
   sliced

This lovely gelatin makes the artificial ingredient-laden, store-bought version hang its head in shame.

Combine ½ cup of grape juice with gelatin in a small bowl and set aside.

Heat remaining juice in a saucepan over medium-low heat for 5 minutes. Add softened gelatin and stir to combine. Add berries, stir, and remove from heat.

Pour into a clear serving dish and refrigerate, uncovered, for 30 minutes, then cover and refrigerate another 3 hours. Serve plain or with whipped cream.

Blueberry Wine Sorbet

Yield: About 1 quart

----

1 pound blueberries
1 cup sugar
½ cup white wine

This dessert tastes much fancier than it is—a gustatory dance between berry and wine.

Combine all ingredients in a blender or food processor and puree. Either freeze in an ice cream maker, according to manufacturer instructions, or freeze in a container, stirring by hand once every 30 minutes until frozen solid, about 5 hours.

Broccoli

Broccoli is the most-loved green vegetable of my household, in no small part because the florets look like little trees for "giant" children to eat. The tough stalks are superior material for Vegetable Stock (*see* page 224), so be sure not to discard them. Broccoli can be eaten raw, stir-fried, steamed, or sautéed, but be careful not to overcook it—ideally broccoli should be bright green with a touch of firmness left.

Broccoli keeps best wrapped in a slightly damp towel in the refrigerator, and can be stored this way for 3 to 4 days before it starts to lose its firmness. To freeze broccoli, blanch for 3 minutes and pack plain or in stock. To dehydrate, dry bite-sized pieces at 130°F for 4 to 10 hours.

Creamy Broccoli Bacon Salad

Serves 4

----

1 pound clean
    broccoli florets
5 slices bacon,
    cooked and
    crumbled
¾ cup mayonnaise
½ cup crumbled
    walnuts
Juice of 1 lime
Zest of 1 lime

This salad turns broccoli into a guilty midnight snack. It's best eaten by the light of the open refrigerator door.

Bring a large pot of salted water to a boil over medium-high heat. Add broccoli florets and boil for 2 minutes. Drain the broccoli and rinse with cold water.

In a serving bowl, combine broccoli with all other ingredients and toss to combine thoroughly. Serve immediately.

Broccoli Peanut Stir-Fry

Serves 4

----

1 tablespoon
soy sauce

1 tablespoon sesame
oil

1 tablespoon
peanut oil

1 pound broccoli
florets, cleaned
and dried

2 cloves garlic,
minced or pressed

1 pound raw,
chopped chicken
or firm tofu

1 tablespoon
chopped peanuts

This dish has plenty of flavour as is, but if you prefer a spicy stir-fry, simply combine a couple of tablespoons of Sriracha (or other hot pepper sauce) with the peanuts.

Combine soy sauce, sesame oil, and peanut oil in a mixing bowl and whisk together.

Heat a sauté pan on medium-high heat. Add liquid mixture and broccoli florets to pan. Sauté, stirring, for 2 minutes, then add garlic and chicken or tofu and continue to sauté, stirring, for another 5 minutes or until all ingredients are cooked through.

Add peanuts, sauté another 30 seconds, and remove from heat. Serve hot with rice.

Broccoli Herb Pasta

Serves 2

----

8 ounces (230 g)
   spaghetti (or any
   other pasta)
2 cups bite-sized
   broccoli florets
   and edible stem
   pieces
¼ cup butter, room
   temperature
¼ cup minced
   fresh herbs
   (parsley, basil,
   thyme, dill,
   cilantro, or a
   combination)
1 tablespoon dark
   miso paste

Full of green things, this healthy pasta is my best dish for carbo-loading
before a long day in the kayak or on the bike trail.

Bring a large pot of salted water to a boil over medium-high heat. Add
pasta and cook until almost tender, 3–5 minutes. Add broccoli and cook
another 2 minutes.

Drain and transfer to a serving bowl. Add butter, minced herbs, and miso
paste, and toss until thoroughly integrated. Serve immediately.

Broccoli Jack Soup

Serves 4

- -

Pure comfort food, this soup is hearty enough for a dinner entrée.

¼ cup butter, room
   temperature
1 large onion, finely
   chopped
2 teaspoons Herb
   Salt (*see* page 120)
   or 1 teaspoon plain
   salt
2 cloves garlic,
   minced or pressed
6 cups Garlic
   Chicken Stock
   (*see* page 107) or
   Vegetable Stock
   (224)
2 pounds broccoli,
   florets and edible
   stems cut into
   bite-sized pieces
1 tablespoon
   cornstarch
1½ cups grated
   Monterey Jack

Combine butter, onion, and salt in a stockpot over medium heat and
sauté, stirring occasionally, until onion is soft, about 10 minutes.

Add garlic and sauté for 1 minute more, then add stock and broccoli.
Bring to a simmer and cook, stirring occasionally, for 5 minutes or until
broccoli is mostly tender but still bright green.

Add cornstarch and Monterey Jack and cook, stirring, until cheese is fully
melted. Serve immediately.

Brussels Sprouts

This vegetable originated near Brussels, Belgium, and only spread throughout Europe and the rest of the world after the First World War. You will often see Brussels sprouts on the stem at the farmers' market—they look like magical staffs with green pompoms. They are actually a kind of miniature cabbage and, like other cabbages, are at their best in cooler weather.

Brussels sprouts are very hearty and can keep in the refrigerator, on the stem, for up to 3 weeks, or loose for up to 10 days. They should be left on the stalk if possible. Wrap either stalks or loose sprouts with a damp towel to store.

Do not overcook Brussels sprouts—both their nutrition and taste will suffer for it. Remove loose leaves before eating. You can cut an "x" in the stem end to allow heat and moisture to penetrate evenly.

To freeze, blanch small heads for 3 minutes and large heads for 5 minutes. Pack plain or in stock. I do not recommend dehydrating Brussels sprouts.

Pecan Brussels Sprouts

Serves 4

¾ cup chopped
    pecans
4 tablespoons butter,
    divided
1 tablespoon
    maple syrup
3 cups thinly sliced
    Brussels sprouts
1 tablespoon
    lemon juice
Salt and pepper
    to taste

Brussels sprouts pair well with the richness of nuts. This recipe coaxes out their full-bodied flavour and is a particularly good accompaniment to pork and poultry entrees.

Preheat oven to 350°F.

In a small saucepan, combine pecans, 2 tablespoons of butter, and maple syrup. Toast over medium heat, stirring constantly, until nuts are toasted and covered with glaze, about 5 minutes. Set aside.

Heat a sauté pan over medium heat. Add remaining 2 tablespoons of butter and sliced Brussels sprouts and sauté, stirring, for 5 minutes. Add lemon juice, glazed nuts, salt, and pepper and sauté for 1 minute more. Serve immediately.

Garlic-Fried Brussels Sprouts

Serves 4

----

1 tablespoon
   peanut oil
4 cloves garlic,
   minced or pressed
2 cups trimmed,
   chopped
   Brussels sprouts
1 teaspoon Herb Salt
   (*see* page 120) or
   ½ teaspoon plain
   salt
Pepper to taste

The cooking time doesn't get shorter than this, nor the Brussels sprouts more tasty. It's all in the heat, so don't be afraid to turn it up high.

Warm the peanut oil in a cast iron skillet over medium heat.

Turn heat between medium-high and high, add garlic and Brussels sprouts, and cook without stirring until edges start to brown, about 2 minutes. Add salt and pepper and stir. Cook another 2 minutes, remove from heat, and serve.

Creamed Chicken and Brussels Sprouts

Serves 4

½ pound mushrooms (any varietal), cleaned and chopped

1 pound Brussels sprouts, cleaned and halved

2 cups cooked, shredded chicken

2¼ cups Garlic Chicken Stock (*see* page 107), divided

Salt and pepper to taste

1 tablespoon minced fresh thyme

1 tablespoon cornstarch

½ cup heavy (35%) cream

2 slices of bread, crumbed

½ cup grated Parmesan

Brussels sprouts have an affinity for Parmesan, which ties all the elements of this dish together for a satisfying, sprouts-heavy entrée.

Preheat oven to 375°F. Butter a 9-by-9-inch baking dish and set aside.

Combine mushrooms, Brussels sprouts, chicken, 2 cups of stock, salt, pepper, and thyme in a mixing bowl.

In a second bowl, whisk remaining ¼ cup of stock with cornstarch and cream. Add to vegetable and chicken mixture and stir to combine.

Transfer to prepared baking dish. Cover evenly with bread crumbs and grated Parmesan. Bake until vegetables are cooked through, about 50 minutes. Cool for 5 minutes, then serve.

Cabbage

According to Cato the Elder, it is the cabbage that surpasses all other vegetables. I don't know if I actually agree with him there, but it *is* a versatile staple throughout the winter months, with a pleasing amount of variety (green, red, Savoy, Napa) to keep you from getting "cabbaged out."

Cabbage is fairly tough when raw, but can be tenderized by generous salting. To tenderize your cabbage before use, slice it thinly then toss with salt—about 1 tablespoon per head. Allow mixture to sit for 2 hours, then rinse and drain. You now have a more tender vegetable that you can use in cooking or eat raw in a salad.

Cabbage can be stored in the crisper drawer or on the counter for up to 1 week. (Use within 1 week if possible.) To freeze cabbage, blanch for 2 minutes and pack plain or in stock. To dehydrate cabbage, slice thinly, blanch for 2 minutes, and dry at 130°F for 12 to 18 hours.

Other recipes using cabbage include Borscht (*see* page 36) and Spicy Lemon Carrot Pickles (58).

Vietnamese Coleslaw

Serves 4–6

If this dish doesn't make you love cabbage, nothing will. Omit the hot pepper sauce if you prefer a less spicy slaw—you won't want for flavour.

¼ cup peanut oil

1 tablespoon toasted
    sesame oil

¼ cup lime juice

2 tablespoons
    Sriracha (or other
    hot pepper sauce)

1 cabbage, cored
    and thinly sliced

1 carrot, peeled
    and grated

½ cup crushed
    roasted peanuts

½ cup minced
    fresh cilantro

Combine peanut oil, toasted sesame oil, lime juice, and hot pepper sauce in a mixing bowl and whisk together vigorously.

In a serving bowl, combine cabbage, carrot, peanuts, and cilantro. Pour dressing over vegetables and toss again. Serve immediately.

Col y Jamon

Serves 4–6

- -

2 tablespoons extra-
virgin olive oil

1 onion, finely
chopped

2 teaspoons Herb
Salt (see page 120)
or 1 teaspoon plain
salt

1 head cabbage
(any varietal),
thinly sliced

2 tablespoons
lemon juice

1 tablespoon cumin

1 teaspoon cayenne

1-pound ham slice,
finely chopped

2 tablespoons
minced cilantro

½ cup sour cream

Spanish for "cabbage and ham," this ingredient pairing is a classic combination in many parts of Mexico. You can use any varietal of cabbage for this recipe, or a combination. You may also use 2 cups of Garlic Pork Shoulder (see page 106) in place of the ham.

Heat the olive oil in a sauté pan over medium heat. Add chopped onion and salt and sauté, stirring occasionally, until onions are soft and golden, about 10 minutes. Add the cabbage, lemon juice, cumin, and cayenne and stir to combine.

Lower heat to medium-low, cover, and simmer mixture until cabbage is cooked through, about 35 minutes.

Add chopped ham and cook for 2 minutes more. Serve topped with minced cilantro and sour cream.

Red Curry Shrimp and Cabbage

Serves 4

- -

1 teaspoon peanut oil

1 tablespoon Thai
red curry paste

5 cups chicken
or fish stock

Zest of 1 lime

Juice of 1 lime

1 pound raw,
deveined,
peeled shrimp

½ of a medium
cabbage, cored
and finely sliced

½ cup chopped
roasted peanuts

½ cup finely
chopped minced
cilantro

This zesty cabbage preparation is inspired by a traditional Asian shrimp pairing.

Heat peanut oil in a large sauté pan over medium heat. Add curry paste and sauté, stirring, for 3 minutes. Add stock, lime zest, and lime juice. Simmer, stirring frequently, for 5 minutes.

Add shrimp and cabbage and cook, stirring, until shrimp is pink and cabbage is wilted, another 4–5 minutes. Serve garnished with peanuts and cilantro.

Parmesan Cabbage Bean Soup

Serves 4

- -

2 tablespoons extra-
  virgin olive oil
1 onion, minced
2 teaspoons Herb
  Salt (*see* page 120)
  or 1 teaspoon plain
  salt
½ medium cabbage
  (any varietal),
  cored and finely
  sliced
6 cups Garlic
  Chicken Stock
  (*see* page 107) or
  Vegetable Stock
  (224)
2 cups cooked beans
1 cup grated
  Parmesan
Pepper to taste

This Italian-style soup serves up a big bowl o' comfort on a chilly, rainy day. Both mild and cheesy, it's popular with the kids.

Combine olive oil, onion, and salt in a stockpot and sauté on medium-low, stirring occasionally, until onion is soft, about 10 minutes. Add cabbage, stock, and cooked beans and bring the soup to a simmer.

Continue to simmer until cabbage is cooked and tender, about 20 minutes. Add Parmesan and pepper and stir until cheese is melted.

Carrots

Recent years have seen a dramatic increase in the availability of carrots in many colours. Of course everyone is familiar with the orange carrot, which was developed as a symbol of Dutch independence in the seventeenth century, but few know that it was cultivated from the sweeter and slightly peppery purple carrot, found today as the varietal Purple Haze. Other carrots include the red carrot, with a taste very similar to the orange carrot, and the sweet, mild, white and golden carrots.

Carrots keep best if you separate the greens from the roots right away. Wash and keep the roots in an open container but covered with a damp towel. The greens, however, should be in an airtight container. Use the washed, chopped greens as an addition to salads.

You can also store carrots upright in a container of clean, damp sand for several months; however, they are very easy to grow and harvest nearly year-round, so why not keep a cold frame (*see* Use What, page 3) of carrots in the garden to harvest fresh throughout the winter? To learn more about how to do this, I recommend reading *The Year-Round Vegetable Gardener* by Niki Jabbour.

To freeze, cook carrots first and pack in stock. To dehydrate, peel, slice, and dry for 6 to 12 hours.

Other recipes using carrots include Borscht (*see* page 36), Garlic Chicken Stock (107), Cream of Leek Soup (125), Lettuce and Bread Soup (130), Curried Potato Soup (178), Radish and Carrot Slaw (183), and Vegetable Stock (224).

Bunny Cupcakes

Serves 12

- -

3 cups all-purpose
flour
2 cups sugar
1 teaspoon salt
1 tablespoon baking
soda
1 tablespoon
cinnamon
1¼ cup coconut oil
4 large eggs
1 tablespoon vanilla
3 cups shredded
carrot
1 cup raisins
1 cup shredded
coconut

If you're crafty, use some Cream Cheese Frosting (*see* below) to pipe a rabbit face onto these delicious cupcakes. They're actually more muffin than cupcake and more healthy than not, but I won't tell your kids if you don't.

Preheat oven to 350°F. Generously grease a muffin tin, or line with cupcake liners, and set aside.

In a mixing bowl, combine flour, sugar, salt, baking soda, and cinnamon. Whisk thoroughly.

In a second bowl, combine coconut oil, eggs, and vanilla. Whisk thoroughly.

Add dry ingredients to wet ingredients and stir to combine. Add shredded carrot, raisins, and shredded coconut and stir again. Transfer batter to prepared tin and bake until a knife inserted in the middle of a cupcake comes out clean, about 45 minutes.

Cool on a rack. Serve plain, or frosted with Cream Cheese Frosting.

Cream Cheese Frosting

Yield: About 2 cups

- -

½ cup butter, room
temperature
8 ounces cream
cheese, room
temperature
1½ teaspoons vanilla
extract
2 cups powdered
sugar

This simple frosting will work for nearly any kind of cake, cupcake, or muffin you will ever bake. Add a teaspoon of cinnamon or cocoa powder or even a splash of liqueur to dress it up!

Combine all ingredients and blend thoroughly.

Spicy Lemon Carrot Pickles

**Yield: approximately
4 pints**

- -

2 pounds carrots,
  peeled and cut
  into thin sticks
1 large head garlic,
  cloves separated
  and peeled
1 jalapeño, chopped
2 teaspoons salt
1–2 cups lemon juice

Even though it consistently makes me feel like a defective food preserver, I
have to confess that I just don't care for vegetables pickled in vinegar. After
I began making refrigerator pickles in lemon juice, however, a new world of
preparation and preservation was revealed.

This recipe can be used to create fresh, crispy pickles with a wide variety
of different vegetables. Simply substitute asparagus, green beans, cabbage,
cauliflower, corn, cucumber, onions, sweet pepper strips, radishes, turnips,
rutabaga, summer squash, or a combination for the carrots. Take out the
garlic and jalapeño, and you can even use it to pickle fruits—try pears with
a cinnamon stick, or a combination of apple slices and cranberry. Keep
in mind that these pickles are not sterile, so they should be stored in the
refrigerator and consumed within 6 weeks.

Pack carrot sticks, garlic cloves, and chopped jalapeño in canning jars
or another clean container with a tight lid. Sprinkle salt on top, then fill
containers to the brim with lemon juice.

Cover tightly and store in the refrigerator for at least a week before
eating. Pickles will keep up to 6 weeks in the refrigerator.

Maple-Glazed Carrots

Serves 4

----

1 pound carrots,
    peeled and sliced
    into thin rounds
2 tablespoons butter
¼ cup maple syrup
½ teaspoon salt
Juice of ½ a lemon
Zest of 1 lemon

This is a fitting side dish for a holiday turkey—not too fussy to make, but impressive for guests, especially if you use multicoloured carrots.

Combine carrots and butter in a sauté pan and sauté, stirring, for 5 minutes. Add maple syrup, salt, and lemon juice, cover, and cook for another 5 minutes. Uncover the pan and cook, stirring, until liquid has mostly evaporated. Remove from heat, sprinkle on zest, and stir to combine. Serve.

Slow-Roasted Carrot Chicken

Serves 6

- -

1 (4–6 pound) whole
   chicken
1 tablespoon salt
1 head garlic,
   separated into
   cloves and peeled
1 bunch thyme,
   parsley, dill
   (or a mix), plus
   2 tablespoons
   minced herbs
10–12 carrots, peeled
   and sliced
2 cups white wine
   or Garlic Chicken
   Stock (*see* page
   107)

If you've never slow-roasted before, you'll be amazed at the tender, moist meat this method produces.

Preheat oven to 280°F. Rinse chicken and rub liberally with salt, inside and out. Stuff body cavity with garlic and bunched herbs and place in a roasting pan.

Combine minced herbs, sliced carrots, and wine or stock in a mixing bowl and gently pour around the outside of the chicken.

Cook until internal temperature of the chicken rises to 150°F, about 3 hours.

Turn temperature up to 400°F and cook until internal temperature of the chicken rises to 165°F and the carrots are tender, about 20 minutes.

Remove from oven and allow chicken to rest for 20 minutes before carving.

Spoon juices over carrots and chicken to serve.

Coconut Curry Carrot Bisque

Serves 6

----

5 pounds carrot,
  peeled and sliced
  into coins

4 cups Vegetable
  Stock (*see* page
  224) or Garlic
  Chicken Stock
  (107)

2 medium onions,
  diced

2 tablespoons extra-
  virgin olive oil

1 teaspoon salt

2–3 tablespoons
  curry powder to
  taste

1 can coconut milk
  (I use organic
  full-fat, but you
  may substitute
  low-fat if you
  wish)

This is a rich, flavourful, and classy soup that can also be vegan when made with Vegetable Stock. Garnish soup with cilantro, fresh grated coconut, an additional sprinkle of curry powder, and/or a decorative carrot peel as desired.

Combine carrot coins with stock, or water and bouillon, in a large stockpot. Bring to a boil over medium-high heat. Reduce heat to low, cover, and simmer until carrots are completely cooked and tender, about 30 minutes.

In the meantime, combine onions, olive oil, and salt in a sauté pan and cook on medium-low, stirring occasionally, until onions are soft and tender, about 25 minutes. Add curry powder during the last couple minutes.

Add onion mixture to the carrots, using a spatula to scrape out all the liquid and spice. Puree the combined mixture with an immersion blender or remove to a stand blender, puree, then return to the pot.

Add coconut milk to puree and stir to blend. Reheat on low for 5 minutes, then serve.

Cauliflower

Cauliflower is not the easiest vegetable to grow, but I think it's one of the most rewarding. Unlike its temperamental cousin, broccoli, cauliflower is nearly impossible to overcook. Braised in stock, it will continue to intensify in flavour up to and including the point where it falls apart into a thick, luscious sauce. While I love the standard white cauliflower, I'm even more enamoured of coloured cauliflowers—orange, purple, and the impossibly beautiful green Romanesco, which looks like a miniature panorama of castle spires.

Cauliflower should be wrapped or otherwise kept in an airtight container. It will keep for up to 1 week, but has the best flavour the day it is cut. To freeze cauliflower, blanch bite-sized pieces for 3 minutes and pack plain or in stock. To dehydrate, dry bite-sized pieces for 6 to 14 hours.

Cauliflower Asiago Soup

- -

1 onion, peeled and
   finely chopped
2 tablespoons butter
2 teaspoons Herb
   Salt (*see* page 120)
   or 1 teaspoon plain
   salt
1 head cauliflower,
   cleaned and
   chopped, tough
   stem discarded
   (fresh, dried
   and rehydrated,
   or frozen and
   thawed)
2 tablespoons
   minced thyme
4 cups Vegetable
   Stock (*see* page
   224) or chicken
   stock
½ cup grated Asiago
½ cup sour cream
Pepper to taste

Although most of my recipes are flexible around substituting herbs, I do not recommend using anything but thyme in this soup. It has an aromatic quality that can't be achieved any other way.

Combine onion, butter, and salt in a stockpot and sauté on medium-low, stirring occasionally, until onion is soft, about 10 minutes.

Add cauliflower, thyme, and stock. Simmer until cauliflower is tender, about 20 minutes. Puree with a stick blender or remove to a stand blender, puree, and return to pot.

Add Asiago cheese, sour cream, and pepper to the soup. Warm over low heat until cheese is melted and thoroughly integrated. Serve immediately.

Garlic Cauliflower Pasta

Serves 4

- - - - - - - - - - - - - - - -

1 head of cauliflower,
   cut into florets,
   inedible parts
   discarded
   (fresh, dried
   and rehydrated,
   or frozen and
   thawed)
1 pound linguine
   (or other pasta)
3 cloves garlic,
   minced or pressed
¼ cup extra-virgin
   olive oil
¼ cup grated
   Parmesan
Pepper to taste

This is one of those recipes that is both consistently satisfying and easy to learn by heart—just what you need at the end of a long day, when everyone's hungry and your brain is full!

Bring a large pot of salted water to a boil over medium-high heat. Add cauliflower and cook until tender, about 10 minutes.

Drain cauliflower, but save water and return it to pot, and return pot to heat. Chop cooked cauliflower finely.

Add pasta to boiling water and cook until tender, about 10 minutes. Drain.

In the meantime, combine garlic and olive oil in a sauté pan over low heat. Sauté, stirring, for 5 minutes.

Combine cauliflower, pasta, garlic mixture, Parmesan, and pepper in the pot and stir to combine. Serve immediately.

Tomato Cauliflower Curry

**Serves 4 as an entrée
or 6 as a side dish**

¼ cup extra-virgin
    olive oil
3 medium tomatoes,
    chopped
2 tablespoons
    minced ginger
1 tablespoon curry
    powder
1 teaspoon salt
1 large or 2 small
    heads cauliflower,
    trimmed florets
    only

As mentioned previously, cauliflower is difficult to overcook, so don't be afraid to let it go a little long. If the cauliflower breaks down it'll be just as delicious, but more like a thick sauce than a chunky vegetable.

Combine olive oil, chopped tomatoes, minced ginger, curry powder, and salt in a pot and sauté over medium-high heat for 5 minutes, stirring frequently.

Add cauliflower and reduce heat to low. Cook until cauliflower is tender when pierced, about 10 minutes. Serve alone, or with rice or pasta as an entrée.

Pan-Asian Cauliflower

Serves 4

- -

2 tablespoons extra-
     virgin olive oil
2 onions, minced
½ teaspoon salt
¼ teaspoon turmeric
2 small or 1 medium-
     large head of
     cauliflower,
     washed and
     trimmed into
     florets (fresh, dried
     and rehydrated,
     or frozen and
     thawed)
2 cloves garlic,
     minced
1 tablespoon Sriracha
     (or other hot
     pepper sauce)
3 tablespoons
     minced cilantro

This recipe will warm your belly and clear the fuzz out of your brain. I use frozen cauliflower to make this dish on grey winter days.

Heat the olive oil in a sauté pan over medium heat. Add onions, salt, and turmeric and cook, stirring occasionally, until onions are soft and golden, about 10 minutes.

Add cauliflower and garlic, cover, and sauté until cauliflower is tender, about 8 minutes. Add hot pepper sauce and cilantro, toss, and serve.

Celery

*G*arlands of celery adorned King Tut's tomb, possibly because this vegetable has always been considered an aphrodisiac. Madame de Pompadour fed celery soup to Louis XV (*Doctor Who* fans, you know what I'm talking about). Unfortunately, that whole "ants on a log" trend bit celery's reputation in the behind. It's time to bring it back.

Of course, as one leg of the classic *mirepoix* (the other two legs are carrot and onion), celery is an essential component to any stock I make. Most people use the stalks and discard the leaves, but in my opinion the leaves are the very best part—I use them as an herb, and especially in Herb Salt (*see* page 120).

Fresh celery can be stored on the counter, upright in a container, with a ½ inch of water. I don't recommend freezing celery. To dehydrate, slice stalks and dry at 130°F for 4 to 12 hours.

Other recipes using celery include Garlic Chicken Stock (*see* page 107), Herb Salt (120), Cream of Leek Soup (125), Fresh Tomato Sauce (207), and Vegetable Stock (224).

Celery in Spicy Vinaigrette

Serves 4–6

- -

Juice of 1 lime
1 tablespoon toasted
   sesame oil
1 teaspoon soy sauce
½ teaspoon red
   pepper flakes
2 large bunches
   celery, cleaned
   and sliced into
   bite-sized pieces

Not many green veggies pair well with the strength of a toasted sesame oil vinaigrette, but celery does it beautifully. Sometimes we get chili chicken at JiXiang on Quinpool Road in Halifax, bring it home, and make this on the side for what I like to call "Extreme Chinese Goodness Hour."

In a serving bowl, combine lime juice, sesame oil, and soy sauce. Whisk thoroughly, add red pepper flakes, and whisk again. Add sliced celery, toss, and serve immediately.

Cream of Celery Soup

- -

1 pound fresh celery,
  washed and thinly
  sliced
2 tablespoons butter
1 onion, minced
1 teaspoon Herb Salt
  (*see* page 120) or
  ½ teaspoon plain
  salt
4 cups chicken stock
  or Vegetable Stock
  (224)
Pepper to taste
1 cup heavy (35%)
  cream

The quality of this soup depends on two things: the quality of the celery and the quality of the stock. It's good enough to be worth making with grocery store produce, but it's phenomenal with fresh, local produce.

Combine the celery, butter, onion, and salt in a stockpot and sauté over medium heat until celery and onion are both soft, about 10 minutes.

Add the stock and simmer for 15 minutes. Remove from heat and either puree with a stick blender or remove to a stand blender, puree, and return to a clean pot.

Add pepper and cream and return to heat until warmed through. Serve with Parmesan.

Celery Gratin

Serves 4

Use your more tender stalks to make this rich dish.

1 tablespoon butter

1 small onion, minced

1 bunch of celery, cleaned and sliced into large bite-sized chunks, leaves reserved

3 teaspoons Herb Salt (*see* page 120) or 1½ teaspoons plain salt

3 cups Vegetable Stock (*see* page 224) or chicken stock

½ cup heavy (35%) cream

Pepper to taste

½ cup grated Parmesan

1 slice of fresh bread, crumbed

¼ cup minced fresh parsley (optional)

Heat oven to 400°F. Butter a baking dish and set aside.

Combine butter, onion, celery, and salt in a sauté pan and sauté on medium-low, stirring occasionally, until vegetables are soft, about 10 minutes. Add stock, cream, and pepper and stir to combine. Transfer to prepared baking dish.

Top vegetable mixture with Parmesan and bread crumbs. Bake until cheese is toasted, about 20 minutes. Cool for 10 minutes, top with minced parsley if desired, and serve.

Corn

Corn gets a bad rap these days, thanks to the mind-boggling amount of genetically modified, monocropped corn that degrades otherwise respectable farmland across Canada and the United States. However, there's little more pleasurable than fresh, sweet corn from a heritage strain, boiled and topped with Herb Butter (*see* page 118), or the condiment of your choice.

One thing corn won't do is keep. The sugars in the kernels start to break down the minute the cob leaves the stalk. Eat it or preserve it the same day if possible, or if not, as soon as you can.

To freeze corn, blanch ears for 5 minutes, cut kernels from cobs, and pack in stock. To dry, first cut kernels from cobs, then dehydrate for 6 to 12 hours.

Corn is also used in Cold Tomato Vegetable Soup (*see* page 208) and can be pickled using the recipe for Spicy Lemon Carrot Pickles (66). Use raw cobs, kernels removed, for Vegetable Stock (224).

Mexican Corn Chowder

Serves 4

- -

4 ears of corn,
    kernels removed
    and cobs reserved
    (fresh, dried
    and rehydrated,
    or frozen and
    thawed)
2 medium potatoes,
    peeled and
    chopped into bite-
    sized pieces
2 cups Garlic Chicken
    Stock (see page
    107) or Vegetable
    Stock (224)
1 onion, finely
    chopped
1 tablespoon butter,
    divided
2 teaspoons Herb
    Salt (see page 120)
    or 1 teaspoon plain
    salt
1 red bell pepper
1 teaspoon cumin
1 teaspoon cayenne
    powder
¼ cup finely
    chopped fresh
    cilantro
1 cup sour cream

Good Mexican food is hard to come by in the Maritimes. Luckily, it's not hard to make your own, as this *sopa caliente* demonstrates.

In a stockpot, combine corn cobs, potato, and stock. Bring to a boil over medium-high heat and cook, stirring occasionally, until potato is cooked through, about 30 minutes. Remove cobs and reduce heat to low.

Meanwhile, combine onion, butter, and salt in a sauté pan and sauté on medium-low, stirring occasionally, until onion is soft, about 10 minutes. Add bell pepper and corn kernels. Continue to sauté until bell pepper is cooked through, about another 10 minutes.

Add vegetable mixture, cumin, and cayenne to stock. Stir to combine and continue to heat on low for 5 minutes. Remove from heat and serve immediately, garnished with cilantro and sour cream.

Corn Bacon Salad

Serves 4

- -

4 slices bacon,
    chopped
4 ears of fresh corn,
    kernels cut from
    ears and cobs
    discarded or saved
    for stock
1 clove garlic, minced
2 cups chopped
    lettuce (any
    varietal)
1 tablespoon extra-
    virgin olive oil
1 tablespoon lime
    juice
1–2 teaspoons
    Sriracha (or other
    hot pepper sauce)

This may be decadent for a salad—but if you're ever going to eat bacon, this is the time.

Fry bacon over medium heat in a cast iron pan. When bacon is almost done, about 10 minutes, turn heat to low, drain off most of the fat, add corn and minced garlic, and sauté, stirring, for 5 minutes. Remove from heat and toss with lettuce.

In a separate bowl, whisk olive oil, lime juice, and hot pepper sauce together. Drizzle over salad, toss, and serve immediately.

Creamed Corn

Serves 6

----

2 tablespoons butter

1 medium onion,
   finely minced

2 teaspoons Herb
   Salt (*see* page 120)
   or 1 teaspoon plain
   salt

Kernels from
   8 ears of corn
   (fresh, dried
   and rehydrated,
   or frozen and
   thawed)

½ cup water

½ cup heavy (35%)
   cream

¼ teaspoon smoked
   paprika

Pepper to taste

Creamed corn is another staple that tastes completely different when homemade. Try it once and you'll never go back to canned.

Combine butter, onion, and salt in a sauté pan and sauté on medium-low, stirring occasionally, until onion is soft, about 10 minutes.

Add corn kernels and water and continue to cook, stirring frequently, until corn is tender, 10–15 minutes.

Add cream, paprika, and pepper and continue to cook, stirring frequently, for another 5 minutes. Remove from heat and serve.

Spicy Corn Fritters

Serves 4

----

1 cup all-purpose
    flour
1 teaspoon Herb Salt
    (*see* page 120) or
    ½ teaspoon plain
    salt
1 teaspoon ground
    cumin
½ teaspoon cayenne
    powder
1 large egg, lightly
    beaten
1 teaspoon lime juice
½ cup water
Kernels from
    3 ears of corn
    (fresh, dried
    and rehydrated,
    or frozen and
    thawed)
1 clove garlic, minced
    or pressed
¼ cup minced
    cilantro
¼ cup peanut oil

Be careful working with the oil in this recipe—you don't want to get burned! I recommend wearing long sleeves and being mindful of oil spatter.

Combine flour, salt, cumin, and cayenne in a mixing bowl. Whisk to combine.

In a second mixing bowl, beat egg, lime juice, and water together. Add corn, garlic, cilantro, and dry ingredients. Blend until just combined.

Heat a sauté pan on medium-high heat. Add peanut oil, then gently place balls of about 1 tablespoon of batter into the oil, leaving 1 inch of space in between them. Cook until browned, about 3 minutes per side.

Drain cooked fritters on a paper towel for a few minutes, then serve immediately with Jalapeño Mayonnaise (*see* page 165).

Cucumber

No vegetable wants to be eaten fresh quite as much as the cucumber. Cucumbers don't dehydrate or freeze well enough to merit the effort, so you'd best make salad while the sun shines. Cucumbers have a bad reputation for making you burp. Most of the chemical responsible is in the ends and the skin, so if you're prone to "cuke burps," cut off both ends and peel.

Cucumbers keep best wrapped in a damp towel in the refrigerator. They'll keep for up to 5 days. If you'll be eating them within a day, they can be kept on a countertop.

Cucumber Salad

Serves 4

----

1 cup plain, full-fat
    yogurt
1 teaspoon Herb Salt
    (*see page 120*)
2 teaspoons minced
    fresh dill or parsley
1 tablespoon lemon
    juice
Pepper to taste
3 fresh cucumbers,
    peeled, quartered,
    and sliced

For this salad, the fat in the yogurt not only boosts flavour—it also helps your body access some of the nutrients in the cucumbers, so don't substitute fat-free. Then again, I consider fat-free yogurt to be a crime against nature in any recipe!

Whisk yogurt, Herb Salt, herbs, lemon juice, and pepper together in a serving bowl. Add cucumber pieces, toss, and serve immediately.

Spicy Cucumber Paletas

Serves 8

----

3 cups chopped,
    peeled, seeded
    fresh cucumber
½ cup sugar
¼ cup lemon juice
½ of 1 jalapeño,
    seeded and
    minced

Cucumbers ripen at the time of summer when you most need a refreshing ice pop. It might sounds like a strange combination at first, but you won't be disappointed when you try this marvellous combination of heat and chill.

Combine all ingredients in a blender and puree.

Pour mixture into an ice pop mould with room for 8. Freeze until firm, about 4 hours.

Cucumber Halibut

Serves 4

----

2 large fresh
   cucumbers,
   seeded, peeled,
   and finely
   chopped
2 tablespoons butter
2 teaspoons lemon
   juice
½ teaspoon Herb Salt
   (*see* page 120) or
   ¼ teaspoon plain
   salt
¼ teaspoon pepper
½ cup Vegetable
   Stock (*see* page
   224) or chicken
   stock
2 teaspoons minced
   dill
2 tablespoons
   minced parsley
2½ cups dry bread
   crumbs
4 halibut filets

This single-dish meal tastes like an ocean breeze feels, and is just as welcome at the end of a summer day.

Preheat oven to 350°F. Butter a baking pan and set aside.

Combine cucumber, butter, lemon juice, salt, and pepper in a sauté pan and cook over medium heat, stirring for 8 minutes. Add stock and continue to cook for another 5 minutes. Remove from heat.

Add dill, parsley, and bread crumbs to vegetable mixture and stir to combine. Transfer half the mixture to prepared baking dish. Place halibut filets in a single layer in the dish, then cover with remaining vegetable mixture. Bake for 25 minutes. Serve immediately.

Cucumber Dill Soup

Serves 4

----

4 medium or 6 small
  cucumbers, peeled
  and chopped,
  large seeds
  removed
½ onion, minced
2 tablespoons lemon
  juice
2 tablespoons
  minced, fresh dill
6 cups Vegetable
  Stock (*see* page
  224)
2 teaspoons Herb
  Salt (120) or
  1 teaspoon plain
  salt
Pepper to taste
1¼ cup plain, full-fat
  yogurt

This soup is especially pretty when garnished with snips of dill and ribbons of cucumber. Prepare it early in the day before the heat clobbers you, then pull it out at lunch or dinner.

Combine cucumbers, onion, lemon juice, dill, stock, salt, and pepper in a stockpot. Bring to a boil over medium-high heat, then reduce heat to medium-low and simmer for 30 minutes. Remove from heat and puree with an immersion blender, or remove to a stand blender, puree, and return to pot. Add yogurt, combine, and chill for at least 3 hours. Serve cold.

Eggplant

Originally cultivated in India, eggplant was first introduced to North America by Thomas Jefferson. As a large vegetable with dense, meaty flesh, it quickly gained popularity on this continent and continues to enjoy a great following today. The taste of the pulp works well with tomatoes and onions. Eggplant is commonly spiced with allspice, basil, bay leaves, oregano, thyme, parsley, and chilies.

When choosing an eggplant, look for firm, heavy fruit with undamaged skin. An eggplant in good condition can be kept on a cool countertop for up to 3 days or in the crisper of the refrigerator for 5 or so. Don't wash until just before use.

To freeze, peel and slice eggplant, blanch for 4 minutes, then pack plain or in stock. To dry, peel, slice, and dry at 130°F for 10 to 18 hours.

Spicy Walnut Eggplant

Serves 4

----

1 large eggplant,
    cut into bite-
    sized pieces
    (fresh, frozen and
    thawed, or dried
    and rehydrated)
1 teaspoon plain salt
2 cloves garlic,
    minced or pressed
1 tablespoon sesame
    oil
1 tablespoon soy
    sauce
1 tablespoon lemon
    juice
2 tablespoons peanut
    oil
1 tablespoon Sriracha
    (or other hot
    pepper sauce),
    optional
1/3 cup chopped
    walnuts

This dish is a game-changer for adults who think they don't like eggplant. I know, I used to be one.

Combine the eggplant and salt in a mixing bowl and toss together. Transfer to a colander and allow pieces to drain for 45 minutes, then pat dry.

In the meantime, preheat oven to 400°F. Toss dry eggplant pieces with garlic, sesame oil, soy sauce, lemon juice, and peanut oil. Roast in a baking dish until eggplant is tender, about 45 minutes.

Remove from oven and toss with hot pepper sauce if desired. Garnish with chopped walnuts. Serve with couscous or rice.

Roasted Miso Eggplant

Serves 4

- -

2 tablespoons lemon
   juice
1 tablespoon extra-
   virgin olive oil
1 tablespoon honey
2 tablespoons miso
2 tablespoons
   Vegetable Stock
   (*see page 224*)
1 large or 2 small,
   fresh eggplants,
   sliced in half
   lengthwise
¼ cup minced
   parsley

If you don't have or don't like miso, you can substitute an equivalent amount
of Parmesan. Eat this dish by itself for a light summer lunch, or with rice and
fish for dinner.

Preheat oven to 375°F.

Combine lemon juice, olive oil, honey, miso, and stock in a mixing bowl
and whisk together. Pierce sliced eggplant with a fork several times along
the sliced surface. Place eggplant in a baking dish, cut-side up, and coat
surface with miso mixture.

Bake until eggplant is completely tender, about 50 minutes. Sprinkle with
parsley and serve immediately.

Eggplant Onion Dip

Serves 4

----

2 large, whole, fresh
   eggplants, washed
   and dried
1 large onion, minced
½ cup olive oil
2 teaspoons Herb
   Salt (*see* page 120)
   or 1 teaspoon plain
   salt
4 cloves garlic,
   minced or pressed
¼ cup lemon juice

This Middle Eastern-influenced dish mixes it up for a summer get-together with friends. Try it with pita chips and fresh garden veggies out on the patio to treat all your senses at once.

Preheat oven to 450°F.

Puncture each eggplant with a fork 4–5 times. Place on a baking sheet and bake for 30 minutes, turning once. Allow to cool for 10 minutes before handling.

Meanwhile, combine the onion, olive oil, and salt in a sauté pan over medium-low heat. Sauté, stirring occasionally, until onion is soft and lightly browned, about 20 minutes. Add garlic and sauté another 2 minutes.

Slice eggplants open and scoop out innards, discarding seeds. Combine eggplant flesh with onion mixture and lemon juice in a blender or food processor. Pulse to puree. Serve warm or room temperature with crackers, bread, chips, or raw vegetables.

Cheesy Eggplant Casserole

Serves 2–3

This rich, easy-to-prepare entrée is a pure comfort food for gardeners.

2 tablespoons extra-virgin olive oil

1 onion, finely chopped

1 teaspoon Herb Salt (*see* page 120) or ½ teaspoon plain salt

1 medium eggplant, peeled and chopped into bite-sized pieces (fresh, frozen and thawed, or dried and rehydrated)

2 thick slices bread, chopped into bite-sized pieces

3 eggs, lightly beaten

1 tablespoon fresh minced parsley, marjoram, thyme, or a combination

1 cup firmly packed, grated cheddar cheese

Preheat oven to 350°F. Butter a baking dish.

Combine olive oil, onion, and salt in a sauté pan and sauté, stirring occasionally, until onion is soft, about 10 minutes. Add eggplant and sauté another 5 minutes.

Combine vegetable mixture with bread, beaten eggs, minced herbs, and grated cheese in a mixing bowl. Transfer to prepared baking dish and bake for 30 minutes. Allow to cool for 5 minutes, then serve.

Eggplant Fries

Serves 4–6

----

1 large (or 2 small)
  fresh eggplant,
  cut into french fry-
  sized sticks
3 teaspoons salt,
  divided
2 cups peanut oil
1 cup pastry flour
1 teaspoon cayenne
  pepper (optional)
1 teaspoon garlic
  powder
1 tablespoon lemon
  juice

Back when I was the mom of a picky toddler, one of my greatest culinary revelations was that kids will eat just about anything that resembles a french fry, even eggplant! Adults like them too. These fries are great with a homemade ketchup or creamy garlic dipping sauce.

Toss eggplant sticks with 2 teaspoons salt in a bowl and cover. Set aside for 2 hours.

Heat peanut oil in a deep pot over medium-high heat.

Meanwhile, combine flour, cayenne powder (if using), garlic powder, and remaining 1 teaspoon salt in a mixing bowl, and whisk to combine.

In a second bowl, combine eggplant sticks with lemon juice and toss. Transfer fries to flour mixture and toss, to coat in batches.

Carefully add coated eggplant sticks to hot oil in batches, and fry until golden-brown, about 5 minutes. Drain on paper towels and serve immediately.

Garlic

Garlic has been used for food and medicine (and, of course, to ward off supernatural creatures) since the dawn of recorded time. In the garden it sends up crunchy, delightful scapes that can be harvested when most other vegetables are still seedlings. In the late summer and early fall, fresh garlic offers itself as medicine for summer colds. Garlic's bite mellows with cooking, so that lightly sautéed garlic is quite strong, while roasted garlic is creamy and mild.

Green garlic can be kept on the counter for a couple of days or in a container in the refrigerator for up to 5 days. Cured garlic should be stored loose in a cool, dark place. It can keep this way for the better part of a year. Because it keeps so well there's little reason to freeze or dehydrate it, but if you wish to do so, you may freeze it by peeling and slicing cloves, immersing them in extra-virgin olive oil, packing, and freezing. You may also slice peeled cloves and dry them at 130°F for 5 to 8 hours. To freeze scapes, cut into bite-sized pieces, blanch for 2 minutes, and pack plain or in stock or oil. To dehydrate scapes, dry at 130°F for 5 to 8 hours.

Walnut Scape Pesto

- -

20–25 garlic scapes,
green parts only,
finely chopped

⅔ cup grated
Parmesan

½ cup extra-virgin
olive oil

1 teaspoon Herb Salt
(*see* page 120) or
½ teaspoon plain
salt

½ cup crumbled
walnuts

Tender, crunchy scapes taste like a cross between garlic and green beans, and they're one of my favourite tastes of spring. Removing scapes from your garlic plants brings their fresh taste into your kitchen early in the season, while maximizing your harvest later in the year—win-win! This pesto keeps beautifully in the freezer and will last in the refrigerator for at least 2 weeks. Tossed with pasta, it makes an easy, fresh, and nutritious meal any time of the year.

Combine all ingredients in a blender or food processor and puree.

Garlic Pork Shoulder

Serves 4–6

2-pound boneless
   pork shoulder
   roast
1 tablespoon Herb
   Salt (*see* page 120)
2 tablespoons extra-
   virgin olive oil
1½ large bulbs garlic,
   cloves separated
   and peeled
1 tablespoon chili
   powder
2 bay leaves

This recipe evolved out of food writer David Lebovitz's spicy *carnitas* recipe from his blog (davidlebovitz.com). The more garlic I added and the less spice, the more my son liked it! Despite the large amount of garlic, the taste in the final dish is mild, and functions as more of an accent than a main focus.

Chop shoulder roast into cubes of meat roughly 4 inches (10 cm). Rub salt into meat cubes, cover, and refrigerate for 1 hour or up to 24 hours.

Preheat oven to 325°F.

Heat a large cast iron pan over medium-high heat. Add olive oil, then carefully place meat cubes in pan. Sear meat on all sides until nicely browned.

Remove from heat and add garlic, chili powder, and bay leaves, and fill pan with water to just below the rim. Transfer pan to oven.

Braise, turning pork occasionally, until meat is very tender and comes apart when poked with a fork, about 3 ½ hours. Remove bay leaves.

Using two forks, break meat down into shreds. Increase heat to 375°F. Return pan to oven for another 30 minutes, remove, and serve.

Garlic Chicken Stock

Yield: approximately 2 litres

- -

3–4 pounds chicken parts

1 onion, quartered

3 celery stalks, roughly chopped

2 carrots, peeled and roughly chopped

2 large or 3 small bulbs garlic, cloves separated and peeled

10 peppercorns

2 bay leaves

2 teaspoons Herb Salt (*see* page 120)

2 litres water

For the chicken parts in this recipe, I recommend using the leftover carcass of a roasted chicken with some of the meat, especially wings and legs, left on. I buy old laying hens from Aaron Hiltz of CanaanLand Pastured Products at my farmers' market for this purpose; the older birds have a more concentrated, full-bodied flavour. If you can get one, use a mature laying hen. Many farmers are thrilled to find buyers for these older, smaller, tougher birds, and the strong flavour of the meat is ideal for a rich, high-quality stock. For a non-garlicky stock, reduce the garlic in the recipe to 2 cloves or omit altogether.

Combine all ingredients in a large stockpot. Bring just to a simmer over medium-low heat. Strain off any froth or scum that bubbles to the top in the first 45 minutes. Continue to simmer until vegetables are very tender and meat is falling off chicken bones, about 3½ hours.

Remove all solids by lifting out large chunks with a slotted spoon, then strain remaining liquid through cheesecloth or a mesh bag.

Refrigerate stock until a congealed layer of fat forms on the surface, about 8 hours. Remove fat. Stock will keep in the refrigerator for 3 days or the freezer for 2 months.

Roasted Garlic Soup

Serves 2

----

4 bulbs garlic, cloves
separated and
peeled
¼ cup extra-virgin
olive oil
1 teaspoon Herb Salt
(*see* page 120) or
½ teaspoon plain
salt
3 cups Garlic Chicken
Stock (*see* page
107) or Vegetable
Stock (224)
1 cup heavy (35%)
cream
½ cup minced, fresh
parsley

This rich soup is a fabulous grace note to celebrate the end of the growing
season as the nights grow chilly. Not surprisingly, it's a terrific match for
Thanksgiving turkey.

Preheat oven to 350°F. Combine garlic, olive oil, and salt in a baking pan
and bake until garlic is golden-brown, about 40 minutes.

Combine roasted garlic with stock in a stockpot over medium-low heat
and simmer for 10 minutes. Puree with a stick blender, or remove to a
stand blender, puree, and return to the pot. Add cream and continue to
simmer for another 5 minutes. Serve hot, with parsley sprinkled on top.

Greens

"Greens" encompass a wide range of leafy crops outside of lettuce. In general, greens are considered to be either hearty or tender. Hearty greens include Swiss chard, beet greens, kale, and mature spinach. The simplest, most basic preparation for these greens is a braise, which gives them a tender quality. To braise, begin by trimming the stems and any other tough or woody bits. Sauté with butter over medium heat a few minutes until wilted, then add a ½ cup of vegetable or chicken stock, cover, and simmer a few minutes until tender. Season to taste with garlic, spices, or lemon juice.

Young, tender greens include baby spinach, baby beet greens, baby kale, arugula, mustard, and a variety of Asian greens such as tatsoi and mizuna. The easiest way to enjoy these greens is to simply toss together a salad with vinaigrette (*see* Making Your Own Vinaigrette, page 110).

Most greens should be stored loose in an airtight container with a damp towel in the refrigerator for a few days. Spinach likes to be in an open container in the refrigerator. Arugula should be stored dry. Wrap washed leaves gently with cloth or paper towel and keep in an open container.

Freeze hearty greens by removing the stems, blanching for 2 minutes, drying, and packing plain or in stock. I do not recommend freezing or dehydrating tender greens. I would also encourage you to consider growing your own greens year-round for fresh ingredients any time—build a simple cold frame (*see* Use What, page 3), seed assertively from early spring through mid-fall, and you're in business!

Kale Chips

Serves 2

- -

1 bunch kale, washed
  and dried
1 tablespoon extra-
  virgin olive oil
1 teaspoon sea salt

To be honest, I struggled with kale for years. It's one of those foods that you
"should" like because it's so very good for you, not to mention easy to grow—
but its toughness and strong flavour were unappealing. Then one day I made
a batch of these kale chips. The next day, I made another batch. The next day,
two batches. By the end of the week I'd decimated the kale in my garden and
bought two new packets of seeds. 'Nuff said.

Preheat an oven to 325°F.

Rip tender parts of the leaves off the thick kale stems, and into bite-sized
pieces. Toss in a large bowl with olive oil and salt. (You may also add
any other seasoning you like, such as lemon juice, Parmesan, or Cajun
spice—personally, I like mine with a bit of lemon and a squirt of hot
sauce!)

Spread kale evenly over a baking sheet. Bake until pieces are crisp, and
edges brown but not burnt, 15–20 minutes.

Green Gumbo

Serves 4–6

¼ cup butter

¼ cup all-purpose
flour

2 large onions,
minced

4 celery ribs, finely
sliced

1 green bell pepper,
cored, seeded, and
chopped

1 red bell pepper,
cored, seeded, and
chopped

4 cloves garlic,
minced

8 cups Garlic
Chicken Stock
(see page 107) or
Vegetable Stock
(224)

1 tablespoon Sriracha
(or other hot
pepper sauce)

3 pounds fresh or
frozen greens,
rinsed, stemmed,
and roughly
chopped

Salt and pepper to
taste

1 tablespoon
cornstarch

You can use a variety of greens or a combination for this entrée, including: spinach, kale, Swiss chard, or mustard greens. Cornstarch takes the place of traditional *filé* in this recipe. If you like, you may add chicken or shrimp—or both—for a more traditional gumbo.

Heat butter in a large stockpot over medium heat. Add flour and cook, stirring, until mixture browns, about 10 minutes. Add onion, celery, peppers, and garlic and cook, stirring often, for another 10 minutes.

Add stock, hot pepper sauce, greens, salt, and pepper.

Reduce heat to medium-low and simmer, stirring occasionally, until greens are cooked through, about 1 hour. Add cornstarch and stir until thoroughly integrated. Serve immediately over rice.

Massaged Kale Salad

Serves 4

----

4 cups clean,
   chopped kale,
   loosely packed
2 tablespoons extra-
   virgin olive oil
1 tablespoon lemon
   juice or Herb
   Vinegar
   (*see* page 122)
1 teaspoon Herb
   Salt (120) or
   ½ teaspoon plain
   salt

Part of what makes kale a unique green is its firm, large-celled leaf structure. You can use this feature to your advantage in one way, by baking it into firm chips in the previous recipe, and in another by physically breaking down the cell boundaries with your hands to create a tenderized green with an outstanding taste.

Toss all ingredients in a serving bowl to combine. With just-washed hands, massage kale firmly until it reduces in volume and seems limp, about 3 minutes. Toss again and serve immediately.

Greens Frittata

This recipe works with spinach, Swiss chard, arugula, mizuna, mustard, mâche, etc.—in fact, nearly every green except kale.

6 large eggs
1 cup shredded
   cheddar
2 tablespoons butter
1 onion, minced
2 teaspoons Herb
   Salt (*see* page 120)
   or 1 teaspoon plain
   salt
1 pound fresh greens,
   rinsed, stemmed,
   and finely
   chopped
2 large tomatoes,
   chopped
Pepper to taste

Position a rack in the upper-third of the oven and preheat it to 350°F. Butter an 8-inch baking dish and set aside.

Beat eggs in a mixing bowl until slightly foamy. Add shredded cheddar and set aside.

Combine butter, onion, and Herb Salt in a sauté pan over medium heat and sauté for 10 minutes. Add greens, tomatoes, and pepper, and reduce heat to low. Sauté for 7 minutes, stirring occasionally. Remove from heat and add mixture to beaten eggs.

Transfer mixture to the prepared baking dish. Bake until egg is set and top is lightly browned, about 20 minutes.

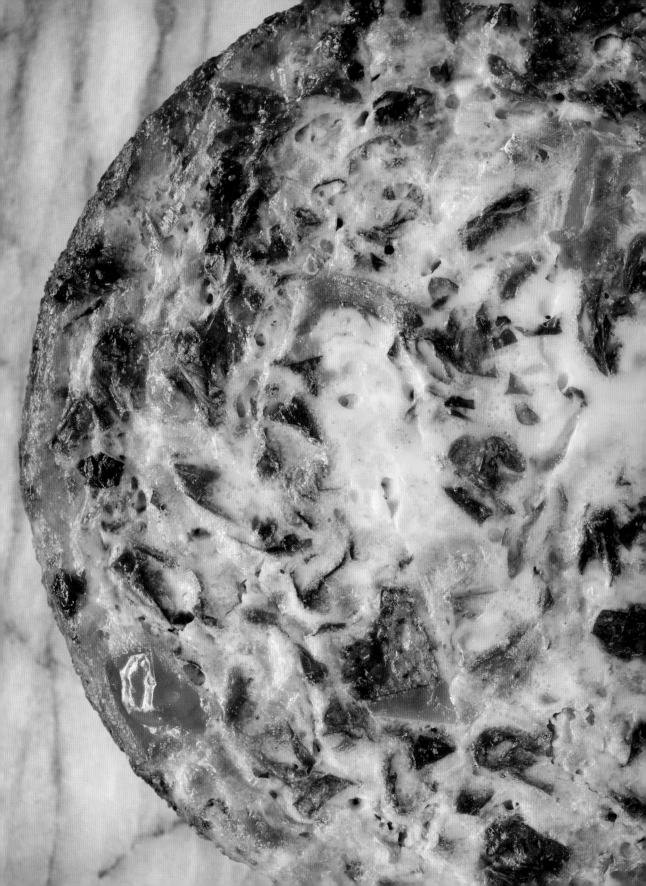

Sesame Garlic Greens

Serves 2

- -

2 tablespoons
   toasted sesame oil
2 cloves garlic,
   pressed or minced
1 tablespoon sesame
   seeds
1 pound fresh greens,
   washed, stemmed,
   and roughly
   chopped
1 tablespoon sugar
   or honey
1 tablespoon soy
   sauce

This recipe is perfect for using Asian greens such as bok choy, mizuna, and tatsoi, but it is also delicious with plain old spinach and Swiss chard.

Heat sesame oil over medium heat in a sauté pan. Add garlic, sesame seeds, and greens, stirring occasionally.

Once the greens are completely wilted, turn heat to low. Add sweetener and soy sauce. Sauté another 2 minutes them remove from heat. Serve hot or cold.

Coconut Curry Greens

Serves 2

- -

1 small onion,
   minced
1 tablespoon peanut
   oil
½ teaspoon plain salt
2 teaspoons curry
   powder
1 pound greens,
   washed and
   chopped
2 tablespoons
   shredded coconut

This Asian take on sautéed greens works particularly well with basic chopped chicken and rice—there's enough flavour in the greens to carry the whole meal.

Combine onion, peanut oil, and salt in a sauté pan and sauté on medium-low, stirring occasionally, until onion is soft, about 10 minutes. Add curry powder and greens and continue to cook, stirring, until greens are limp but still bright green, about another 10 minutes. Add coconut, stir, and serve.

Herbs

Fresh herbs make the difference between "meh" and marvellous in more meals than I care to count. If you only wish to grow a bit of something yourself, I strongly recommend that you choose herbs. Most grow very well on a windowsill year-round—you don't even need to go outside! Add them, chopped, to salads, scrambled eggs, sauces, and as a garnish on nearly everything else.

Common garden herbs include: basil, chives, cilantro, dill, lavender, lemon balm, marjoram, mint, oregano, parsley, rosemary, sage, summer savory, tarragon, and thyme. You can store nearly any fresh herb by treating it like a bouquet of flowers—snip a bit off the stems and stick them in a glass of water. Alternatively, most fresh herbs can be kept in the refrigerator in a closed container for up to 1 week. Basil should be kept cool, if you can manage, but do not store it in the refrigerator, and use within a day if possible. Basil leaves should be kept whole until just before using, as the leaves blacken quickly.

The majority of herbs can simply be air-dried. Arrange clean, dry herbs very loosely in paper bags that are partially closed, still allowing a bit of ventilation. Most herbs will dry in about 2 weeks. The exceptions to this air-drying process are basil, mint, lemon balm, and tarragon. These herbs have a higher-than-normal moisture content and can mould if left to air-dry. Instead, dry these herbs in a food dehydrator at a relatively low heat (about 95°F) for 2 to 4 hours. Package dried herbs in airtight jars.

Keep dried herbs as whole as you can until you are ready to use them, then crumble just before adding to food for maximal flavour. You'll never go back to store-bought herbs again.

I rarely freeze herbs, but if you wish to do so immerse freshly minced herbs in water, oil, or stock in ice cube trays. After cubes have frozen, transfer to a freezing bag until ready to use. This method helps keep the herbs fresh and flavourful while preserving them in easy-to-measure portions.

Herb Butter

Yield: ¾ cup

- -

½ cup butter, room
    temperature
½ cup minced herbs:
    cilantro, basil,
    thyme, parsley,
    dill, rosemary, or a
    combination
2 tablespoons lemon
    or lime juice

Herb butter is one of the easiest ways to make the most of your fresh herbs. Put it on toast, baked potatoes, pasta, rice, corn on the cob, or nearly any other savoury food. If you want to be fancy about it, use a mould to make a pretty-shaped butter. If you aren't using salted butter, add a teaspoon of salt to this recipe.

Mix all ingredients in a mixing bowl, shape in a log, wrap in plastic wrap, and refrigerate. Shape by hand or with cookie cutters if desired. Herb butter will keep up to 5 days in the refrigerator or 3 months in the freezer.

Herb Salt

Yield:
approximately 1 cup

¾ cup sea salt
2 cups stemmed and
    roughly chopped
    herbs

You can use a wide variety of herbs, or combinations of herbs, in this recipe. I'm partial to a blend of oregano, cilantro, and thyme, but you can also use sage, rosemary, summer savory, dill, celery leaves, fennel fronds, or parsley. Use Herb Salt instead of plain salt for seasoning nearly any savoury dish.

Combine sea salt and herbs on a cutting board and mince, continually mixing them together as you work with the knife. Spread mixture on a baking sheet and leave in a warm, dry place for 2 to 3 days, stirring occasionally, until completely dry. Store in closed containers. Salt will keep for 6 months or longer.

Lavender Sugar

Yield: 1 cup

1 cup sugar
1 tablespoon dried
    lavender

Lavender sugar is excellent sprinkled on fruit, as a sweetener for tea, or used in baked goods such as shortbread cookies. Packaged in an attractive container with a bit of ribbon or a handmade tag, it also makes an excellent—and affordable—food gift. You may also use this method to make a mint, rosemary, tarragon, or lemon balm sugar.

Combine sugar and dried lavender in an electric grinder, food processor, or mortar, and grind until lavender is a powder and is mixing evenly throughout sugar. Sugar will stay pungent for up to 8 months.

Herb Pesto

Serves 4–6

- -

2 cups rinsed,
    packed herbs
    (basil, cilantro,
    parsley, thyme, or
    tarragon)
½ cup grated
    Parmesan
½ cup extra-virgin
    olive oil
⅓ cup chopped nuts
2 large cloves garlic,
    minced or pressed
    (optional)
Salt and pepper to
    taste

Pine nuts and basil are the most traditional pesto combination, but really you can use a wide variety of herb and nut combinations with success. I like walnuts and pecans, but I've also had great pestos made with hazelnuts, almonds, and sunflower seeds. Experiment with your favourites! This recipe is best made in a food processor; however, if you don't have one you can use a stand blender or stick blender and still achieve satisfactory results.

Enjoy pestos with pasta; spread on slices of toast; as a spread on meats, or on baked potatoes.

Combine all ingredients in a food processor or blender. Puree, stopping often to scrape the sides and make sure the mixture is evenly pureed. Add salt and pepper and pulse again. Pesto will keep in the refrigerator for 2 weeks or in the freezer for 6 months.

Lime Herb Marinade

Yield: 1 cup

- -

1 cup mixed finely
    chopped herbs
    (any combination
    of parsley, thyme,
    rosemary, cilantro,
    and dill)
5 cloves garlic,
    roughly chopped
¼ cup lime juice
¾ cup extra-virgin
    olive oil

Soak virtually any piece of fish, chicken, or red meat in this marinade for a few hours before baking or grilling for an intensely fresh, savoury flavour. Use whatever herbs you have in your garden or experiment with combinations—I especially like a mixture with at least ⅓ fresh, curly parsley. One cup is about the right amount for marinating 4 servings of meat. You may also use this mixture as a salad dressing. Toss with corn and pasta for a picnic standout!

Combine all ingredients in a blender or food processor and puree. Marinade will keep, covered, in the refrigerator for 1 day if you wish to prepare it ahead of time.

Herb Vinegar

- -

1½ cups white
    vinegar
1 cup fresh herbs,
    rinsed, stemmed,
    and lightly packed

Good choices for an herb vinegar include basil, cilantro, dill, rosemary, sage, summer savory, tarragon, and thyme. You may also add whole peppercorns or garlic cloves to taste. If herbs look wilted or unappetizing, you may strain them out and continue to use the vinegar. Herb Vinegar is lovely in homemade salad dressings, and as an acidic substitute in any recipe that calls for lemon or lime juice.

Bring vinegar to a boil in a saucepan. In the meantime, arrange herbs in a clean glass container. Carefully pour boiling-hot vinegar over herbs. Cool, seal, and store in the refrigerator for at least 2 weeks before using. Vinegar will keep in the refrigerator for several weeks.

Leeks

eeks have been a part of the human diet since antiquity. The Roman emperor Nero is said to have eaten them daily. In 1620 Welsh soldiers placed leeks in their caps so they could easily be differentiated from the Saxons they were fighting.

Leeks are related to onion and garlic, and can be used in similar ways in many recipes. Harvest or buy leeks that are 1½ inches in diameter or less, feature dark green leaves, and firm, white necks. Wild leeks, known as "ramps," are especially delicious. If you see some at the market, snap them up!

Store raw, unwashed leeks in the refrigerator for up to 1 week. Leeks keep best in an open container in the crisper with a damp towel. To use leeks, cut off the tough green tops and reserve for stock. Slice off the root and cut leeks in half lengthwise. Rinse well under cold, running water. Now you can slice and dice them for use in cooking. Unused, clean leek parts are excellent for use in Vegetable Stock (*see* page 224).

I do not recommend freezing leeks, although I do like them dried for quick addition to soups, stews, and salads. To dehydrate leeks, slice, wash, and dry for 12 to 18 hours.

Cream of Leek Soup

Serves 6

- - - - - - - - - - - - - - - - - - -

This mild but flavourful soup is good for whatever ails you.

10 medium-sized
leeks, white and
pale-green parts
only, chopped and
washed
1 onion, finely
chopped
3 carrots, peeled and
sliced
3 celery ribs, sliced
3 teaspoons Herb
Salt (*see* page 120)
or 1½ teaspoons
plain salt
½ cup butter
1 cup white wine
5 cups Garlic Chicken
Stock (*see* page
107) or Vegetable
Stock (224)
1 bay leaf
2 tablespoons
cornstarch
1 cup heavy (35%)
cream
Pepper to taste

Combine leeks, onion, carrots, celery, Herb Salt, and butter in a stockpot and sauté over medium heat for 10 minutes.

Add wine, stock, and bay leaf and bring to a simmer. Continue to simmer, stirring occasionally, until vegetables are cooked through, about 20 minutes. Remove bay leaf.

Remove ½ cup of liquid to a mixing bowl, whisk in cornstarch, and set aside.

Puree soup mixture with an immersion blender or remove to a stand blender, puree, and return to pot.

Add cornstarch mixture, cream, and pepper and return to a simmer, stirring frequently. Serve immediately.

Leek Herb Spread

Serves 4

- -

2 tablespoons extra-
virgin olive oil
2 large or 3 small
leeks, sliced and
cleaned, white and
pale-green parts
only
2 cloves garlic, finely
chopped
1 teaspoon Herb Salt
(*see* page 120) or
½ teaspoon plain
salt
½ teaspoon pepper
¼ cup Vegetable
Stock (*see* page
224) or Garlic
Chicken Stock (107)
2 teaspoons fresh
rosemary or thyme,
finely minced
½ cup cream cheese

A great, simple meal on toast, or an appetizer on crackers or crusty French bread, this recipe shows leeks off to their best advantage.

Combine olive oil, leek, garlic, Herb Salt, and pepper in a sauté pan over medium heat and sauté for 8 minutes.

Turn off heat, add stock to pan, and scrape down sides and water to get all of the brown material into the liquid. Transfer mixture to a mixing bowl.

Add herbs and cream cheese to leek mixture and mash together with a fork. Serve immediately, or refrigerate and serve cold.

Frizzled Leeks

Serves 4

----

1 cup peanut oil

3 large or 5 small
   leeks, cleaned and
   finely chopped

1 teaspoon Herb Salt
   (*see* page 120) or
   ½ teaspoon plain
   salt

On top of a plain steak, chicken breast, omelette, or vegetable casserole, frizzled leeks add textural interest and a boost of flavour. Most children are thrilled to hear that this dish technically counts as a "vegetable."

Heat oil in a saucepan over medium-high heat. Gently add chopped leeks in batches. Fry each batch until golden-brown, about 1 minute.

Transfer fried leeks to paper towels and sprinkle with Herb Salt.

Lettuces

*L*ettuces have been in cultivation for around five thousand years, and the traditional salad preparation (lettuce+oil+vinegar) has been popular since Roman times. There are over one thousand varietals on the market. Whether you prefer leaf, romaine, crisp, or butterhead, lettuce is an energizing food that hits the spot on summer days when you just can't bring yourself to turn the oven on.

Lettuces can be kept in the refrigerator for several days, in an airtight container with a damp towel. Unlike heartier greens, they do not freeze or dry well, so you'll just have to eat them up!

MAKING YOUR OWN VINAIGRETTE

When it comes to vinaigrette, Niki Jabbour, author of *The Year-Round Vegetable Gardener*, passes on this wisdom: "My Lebanese mother-in-law taught me that all salads are best with a simple dressing: olive oil, lemon juice and a sprinkle of salt. Keep in fridge in a jar and it will keep for a week for daily salads." You don't have to follow these instructions to a T in your salad making (although I usually do), but the general principle applies. To make any vinaigrette, whisk together 1 part acid (any vinegar, rhubarb juice, lemon juice, or lime juice) to 3 parts oil (extra-virgin olive oil or a high-quality nut oil). Add flavourings to taste, such as chopped fresh herbs, garlic, spices. Your imagination's the limit here! Toss your dressing with the greens and any nuts, seeds, shredded cheeses, dried fruit, or additional raw vegetables. Voila! Salad completely from scratch.

Lettuce and Bread Soup

Serves 4

----

2 cloves garlic,
    minced or pressed
3 tablespoons extra-
    virgin olive oil,
    divided
4 cups Vegetable
    Stock (*see* page
    224) or Garlic
    Chicken Stock
    (107)
2 carrots, peeled and
    sliced
2 cups stale bread,
    cut into bite-sized
    croutons
1 tablespoon Herb
    Salt (*see* page 120)
    or ½ tablespoon
    plain salt
6 cups lettuce (any
    varietal)
¼ cup chopped
    parsley
¼ cup chopped basil
    or cilantro
Freshly ground
    pepper to taste

You might properly call this "Herb Soup"—lettuce, carrots and bread provide
the structure, while herbs and garlic imbue every drop with flavour.

Preheat oven to 350°F. Combine the garlic and half the olive oil in a
stockpot and sauté over medium heat for 2 minutes.

Add stock and carrot to the pot and simmer, uncovered, for 20 minutes.

In a mixing bowl, toss the croutons with the remaining olive oil and salt.
Transfer to a baking sheet and toast for 20 minutes.

Add lettuce, parsley, and other herbs to soup. Simmer for 10 minutes.
Add pepper to taste. Serve with croutons placed gently on top of the
bowls.

Spicy Lettuce Stir-Fry

Serves 4

- -

1 tablespoon lime
   juice
1 tablespoon soy
   sauce
2 tablespoons peanut
   oil
1 tablespoon Sriracha
   (or other hot
   pepper sauce)
4 cloves garlic,
   minced or pressed
1 pound crisp lettuce,
   washed and
   chopped

Layer this dish with strips of roasted vegetables, pork loin, or pan-fried tofu for a satisfying main dish, or serve as a side for a memorable "hot salad."

Combine lime juice, soy sauce, peanut oil, and hot pepper sauce in a mixing bowl and whisk together.

Heat a sauté pan on high heat. Add sauce mix, garlic, and lettuce and stir-fry, stirring constantly, for 3 minutes or until lettuce is limp but still bright green. Remove from heat and serve.

Mustardy Lettuce

Serves 4

- -

1½ tablespoons
 lemon juice
1 tablespoon mustard
 sauce
1 teaspoon Herb Salt
 (*see* page 120) or
 ½ teaspoon plain
 salt
¼ cup extra-virgin
 olive oil
Pepper to taste
1 pound lettuce
 (any varietal or
 a combination),
 washed and
 roughly chopped

Normally a salad is a lighter flavour on the side of a more heavily spiced entrée, but sometimes your taste buds welcome a little role reversal. This is my go-to salad when I want to pack a little extra punch on the side.

Combine lemon juice, mustard sauce, Herb Salt, olive oil, and pepper in a mixing bowl and whisk vigorously until thoroughly combined. Combine dressing with lettuce in a serving bowl, toss, and serve immediately.

Mushrooms

My warning to never eat wild, foraged produce unless you are confident in your identification goes quadruple for mushrooms. Many culinary mushrooms have an evil twin in the woods just waiting to punish you for your hubris should you get carried away with nature's bounty. On the other hand, mushroom spore kits are available at most garden centres and are an excellent way to produce your own.

Mushrooms dehydrate very well. Slice and dry at 130°F for 3 to 5 hours. Freezing is a little more complicated. To freeze, cut mushrooms into bite-sized pieces, dunk in a solution of 1 tablespoon lemon juice and 2 cups water, steam for 5 minutes, and pack plain or in stock.

Other recipes containing mushrooms include Creamed Chicken and Brussels Sprouts (*see* page 57) and Green Onion Egg Drop (143).

Cream of Mushroom Soup

Serves 4

- - - - - - - - - - - - - - - - - - -

1 pound mushrooms,
  cleaned and diced
  (fresh, frozen and
  thawed, or dried
  and rehydrated)
2 tablespoons flour
4 tablespoons butter,
  divided
1 onion, minced
2 teaspoons Herb
  Salt (*see* page 120)
  or 1 teaspoon plain
  salt
2 cups Vegetable
  Stock (*see* page
  224) or chicken
  stock
¼ cup sherry
1 bay leaf
1½ cups light (10%)
  cream (or ½ cup
  heavy [35%] cream
  and 1 cup whole
  milk)

The little bit of sherry in this recipe makes all the difference.

Heat a sauté pan on medium-high heat. Add diced mushrooms and half the butter and sauté, stirring frequently, until mushrooms are browned and cooked through, about 5 minutes.

Combine remaining butter, onion, and salt in a stockpot and sauté on medium-low, stirring occasionally, until onion is soft, about 10 minutes.

Add stock, half of mushrooms, and puree with a stick blender or remove to a stand blender, puree, and return to the pot. Add remaining half of browned mushrooms to the puree.

Return to heat and sprinkle in flour while stirring. Add sherry and bay leaf and simmer on medium-low for 15 minutes. Remove bay leaf, add cream, and serve.

Stuffed Mushrooms

Serves 4–6

- -

½ cup shredded
Monterey Jack
2 tablespoons grated
Parmesan
2 tablespoons white
wine
2 cloves garlic,
minced or pressed
2 tablespoons sliced
almonds
2 tablespoons
minced parsley
2 teaspoons minced
thyme
2 tablespoons melted
butter
2 tablespoons bread
crumbs
2 dozen fresh
medium-large
mushrooms,
cleaned and
stemmed

These won't wait once they're baked, so eat them hot and fresh! The stuffing can be prepared ahead of time for easy party prep.

Preheat oven to 375°F. Lightly grease a baking sheet and set aside.

Combine cheeses, white wine, garlic, sliced almonds, parsley, thyme, butter, and bread crumbs in a blender and pulse to a pasty consistency. If mixture seems dry, add another tablespoon of wine and blend again.

Fill each mushroom cap with stuffing and place, stuffing side up, on the baking sheet. Bake for 25 minutes. Allow to cool for 5 minutes, then serve.

Mushroom Pâté

Serves 4

----

3 tablespoons butter

2 teaspoons Herb
   Salt (*see* page 120)
   or 1 teaspoon plain
   salt

1 small onion,
   minced

1 clove garlic, minced
   or pressed

½ pound mushrooms
   (any varietal or
   a combination),
   washed and
   minced (fresh,
   frozen and
   thawed, or dried
   and rehydrated)

2 tablespoons
   crushed walnuts

Pepper to taste

1 tablespoon white
   wine

2 tablespoons sour
   cream

1 tablespoon lemon
   juice

1 tablespoon minced
   parsley

The meaty quality of mushrooms comes to the fore in this recipe. An impressive party dish, it will capture the enthusiasm of vegetarians and carnivores alike.

Put a sauté pan on medium-high heat. Add butter, salt, onion, garlic, and mushrooms. Sauté, stirring frequently, until all ingredients are well done, about 8 minutes.

Add walnuts and pepper and sauté for an additional 2 minutes. Remove from heat and allow to cool for 10 minutes.

Add wine, sour cream, lemon juice, and parsley. Mix thoroughly and refrigerate. Serve cold with wheat or rice crackers.

Chicken with Mushroom Wine Sauce

Serves 4

- -

2 tablespoons extra-
virgin olive oil

4 cups cleaned,
stemmed, sliced
mushrooms
(any varietal;
fresh, frozen and
thawed, or dried
and rehydrated)

2 teaspoons Herb
Salt (*see* page 120)
or 1 teaspoon plain
salt

1 pound raw skinless
boneless chicken,
chopped into bite-
sized pieces

2 cloves garlic,
minced or pressed

Pepper to taste

1 cup white wine

1 tablespoon
cornstarch

¼ cup heavy (35%)
cream

Mushrooms and wine complement each other beautifully. Garnish this dish with a little grated Parmesan and chopped parsley if you wish. You may also make the sauce portion of this recipe with red wine as a topping for steak.

Heat a sauté pan over medium-high heat. Add olive oil and sliced mushrooms, and Herb Salt. Sauté, stirring frequently, until mushrooms begin to brown and make a squeaking sound when you stir.

Add chicken pieces and continue to sauté until chicken is browned on the outside. Reduce heat to medium-low, add garlic and pepper, and sauté for 1 minute more.

Add wine and cook, stirring often, for 5 minutes. Add cornstarch and stir to dissolve. Add cream and stir, then remove from heat. Serve immediately with rice, couscous, or mashed potatoes.

Onions

The onion is the most popular allium, and one of the most versatile. I use them in approximately half the savoury dishes I cook! You can caramelize onions for a sweet taste, lightly pan-fry them for a sharp one, or sauté them low and slow for a mild, yet still distinctively oniony flavour. In addition to the cured bulbs, green onions convey freshness and flavour.

Spring onions can be stored loose in the crisper for up to 5 days. Fresh onions can be kept on the counter for a couple of days or in a container in the refrigerator for up to 5 days. Cured onions should be stored loose in a cool, dark place, and can keep this way for several months. You can cure your own onions by hanging them outdoors or arranging them in a single layer on a screen in dry, sunny weather. Once the roots become noticeably harder, 1–2 days, move them to a cool, dry place and remove the tops, leaving about 1 inch attached to the bulb. They will finish curing in this state and can then be simply left alone for storage.

I don't recommend the taste or texture of frozen onions—and given how well they keep when cured, I see little point in trying. To dry, slice and dehydrate for 6 to 12 hours.

Onion Jam

Yield: About 1 quart

- -

¼ cup butter
6 cups peeled and
    thinly sliced
    onions
1 teaspoon salt
1 cup sugar
1 cup balsamic
    vinegar
2 cups red wine

This savoury jam is an apt condiment for many meats. I like it with smoked salmon and cream cheese on bagels.

Combine butter, onions, and salt in a large saucepan.

Cook, stirring occasionally, over low heat until onions turn soft and brown, about 45 minutes.

Add sugar, balsamic vinegar, and red wine and cook, stirring occasionally, until liquid has the consistency of maple syrup.

Remove from heat and refrigerate in jars. Jam will keep for up to 1 month in the refrigerator.

Onion Bread Pudding

Serves 6

- -

½ cup butter

8 cups thinly sliced
    onions (any
    varietal)

1 tablespoon Herb
    Salt (*see* page 120)
    or 2 teaspoons
    plain salt

¾ cup whole milk

¾ cup heavy (35%)
    cream

1 clove garlic, minced
    or pressed

3 large eggs

6 cups bite-sized
    pieces French
    bread

4 cups grated Swiss
    cheese

It's not always easy to make a main dish out of onions, but this versatile bread pudding does the trick. Try it for brunch with a fresh fruit platter!

Preheat oven to 400°F. Generously butter a baking dish and set aside.

Combine butter, onions, and salt in a large saucepan. Cook, stirring occasionally, over low heat until onions turn soft and brown, about 45 minutes.

In a mixing bowl, whisk milk, cream, garlic, and eggs together. Add bread and gently submerge in liquid mixture. Add onions and grated cheese and stir to combine.

Transfer to prepared baking dish. Bake until top is toasted brown, about 40 minutes. Allow to cool for 10 minutes, then serve.

Green Onion Egg Drop

Serves 4

- -

6 cups Vegetable
　　Stock (*see* page
　　224) or chicken
　　stock
1½ cup thinly sliced
　　green onions
1 cup thinly sliced
　　mushrooms
　　(any varietal;
　　fresh, dried and
　　rehydrated,
　　or frozen and
　　thawed)
2 teaspoons soy
　　sauce
2 large eggs
Pepper to taste

This light, easy soup is loaded with springy, oniony goodness. It makes a perfectly refreshing snack or lunch, with a punch of protein to help you push through the afternoon.

Combine stock, green onions, mushrooms, and soy sauce in a saucepan over medium-high heat and bring to a boil. Reduce heat to medium-low and simmer for 5 minutes.

While soup simmers, lightly beat eggs in a bowl. Drizzle eggs into soup, stirring. Cook for 1 additional minute. Add pepper to taste, and serve immediately.

Onion Rings

Serves 4

----

1 tablespoon chili
   powder
1½ cups all-purpose
   flour
2 teaspoons Herb
   Salt (*see* page 120)
   or 1 teaspoon plain
   salt
2 large onions, sliced
   into rings
1 cup light (10%)
   cream
2 cups peanut oil

I like these with Jalapeño Mayonnaise (*see* page 165). If you want to add some spice right in the onion rings themselves, add a teaspoon of cayenne or hot paprika to the flour mix.

Combine chili powder, flour, and salt in a mixing bowl and whisk together thoroughly. Dip onion rings in flour mixture then set aside on a plate.

Pour cream into a second bowl. Dip floured onion rings into cream, then into flour mixture. Set coated rings aside on a fresh plate.

Heat peanut oil in a deep frying pan over medium-high heat. When oil is hot, carefully lower in onion rings and fry, turning once, until golden brown, about 5 minutes. Drain on paper towels and serve hot.

Parsnips

A close relative of parsley with a root like a turnip, the parsnip is a winter vegetable that gets sweeter with cold weather. In fact, the farther north they're planted, the larger they grow. Although parsnips are usually both tougher and sweeter than carrots, they are close in size and appearance and can be cooked quite similarly. If substituting one for the other in a recipe, keep in mind that carrots take slightly longer to cook than parsnips due to their lower sugar content. Unlike with carrots, however, you should not eat parsnip greens—in fact, if you're growing your own, you should avoid touching them with your bare hands as their juice can cause blistering on the skin.

Parsnips keep best if you separate the greens from the roots right away. Wash and keep the roots in an open container but covered with a damp towel. You can store parsnips upright in a container of clean, damp sand for several months.

To freeze parsnips, cook thoroughly first, then pack in stock. To dehydrate, peel, slice, and dry at 130°F for 6 to 12 hours. Parsnips make an excellent addition to Vegetable Stock (*see* page 224).

Parsnip Chips

Serves 4

----

2 cups peanut oil

5 medium or 3 large
   fresh parsnips,
   peeled and thinly
   sliced

2 teaspoons Herb
   Salt (*see* page 120)
   or 1 teaspoon plain
   salt

It's important to slice the parsnips as thinly as you can for this recipe. You can do it successfully by hand, but if you have a mandoline, use it! This recipe is a good use for the larger and slightly tougher parsnips. If your parsnips are too tough and woody to slice thinly, however, save them for Vegetable Stock (*see* page 224) instead.

Line a plate with paper towels and set aside. Heat peanut oil in a heavy saucepan over medium heat.

Carefully add sliced parsnips to heated peanut oil and fry, stirring frequently, until edges are golden, 1–2 minutes. Remove fried parsnips with a slotted spoon to prepared plate. Drain, then sprinkle with salt. Serve warm.

Chicken and Parsnips with Rosemary

Serves 4

----

2 tablespoons extra-
    virgin olive oil
8 medium parsnips,
    peeled and diced
    (fresh, frozen and
    thawed, or dried
    and rehydrated)
1 pound chopped,
    raw chicken
2 tablespoons butter
1 tablespoons fresh
    minced rosemary
2 teaspoons Herb
    Salt (*see* page 120)
    or 1 teaspoon plain
    salt
1 tablespoon honey
Pepper to taste

Parsnips and rosemary have a great affinity for one another; the honey in this dish accentuates the flavours of both ingredients.

Heat a large sauté pan over medium-high heat. Add olive oil, diced parsnips, and chopped chicken. Sauté, stirring, until both chicken and parsnips are browned and cooked through, about 15 minutes.

Reduce heat to medium; add butter, rosemary, salt, honey, and pepper and continue to cook, stirring, for 5 minutes. Serve immediately.

Walnut Maple Parsnips

Serves 4

- -

4 cups peeled,
sliced parsnips
(fresh, frozen and
thawed, or dried
and rehydrated)
4 tablespoons butter,
melted
⅓ cup maple syrup
1 clove garlic, minced
2 teaspoons Herb
Salt (*see* page 120)
or 1 teaspoon plain
salt
Pepper to taste
¾ cup crushed
walnuts

You can substitute a cooking oil for the butter in this recipe to make it vegan if desired—I recommend a nut oil, such as hazelnut, almond, or, of course, walnut.

Preheat oven to 375°F and generously butter a baking dish.

Combine parsnips, butter, maple syrup, garlic, salt, and pepper in a mixing bowl, toss, and transfer to baking dish. Bake until parsnips are tender, about 1 hour.

Top with crushed walnuts and bake another 10 minutes. Cool for 5 minutes and serve.

Ginger Parsnip Cake

Serves 8

1½ cups all-purpose
    flour
1 tablespoon ground
    ginger
2 teaspoons baking
    powder
2 teaspoons ground
    cinnamon
¾ teaspoon salt
¾ cup honey
3 large eggs
½ cup melted butter
½ cup ginger ale or
    ginger beer
2 teaspoons vanilla
2 cups shredded
    peeled parsnips
    (fresh, frozen and
    thawed, or dried
    and rehydrated)
¾ cup golden raisins

Even though most people know that you can use parsnips in the same way you use carrots, it still comes as a surprise, even to carrot cake lovers, to think of a parsnip cake! I would argue, however, that parsnips are an even better vegetable for sweet baking than carrots because they themselves are sweeter. It's extra-important to use smaller, more tender parsnips for this recipe to give the cake the right texture.

Preheat oven to 350°F. Generously butter a loaf pan and set aside.

Combine flour, ginger, baking powder, cinnamon, and salt in a mixing bowl and whisk to combine.

In a second mixing bowl, combine honey, eggs, butter, ginger ale or beer, and vanilla and whisk thoroughly. Add shredded parsnips and raisins and stir to combine.

Add dry ingredients to wet ingredients and stir until thoroughly combined. Transfer batter to prepared loaf pan. Bake until a knife inserted in the centre comes out clean, about 35 minutes.

Cool in the pan on a rack. Serve plain, dusted with powdered sugar, or with Cream Cheese Frosting (*see* page 65).

Caramelized Parsnip Soup

Serves 4

----

2 tablespoons butter

1 medium onion, chopped

½ teaspoon salt

1 pound parsnips, peeled and cubed (fresh, frozen and thawed, or dried and rehydrated)

1 clove garlic, finely chopped

½ cup maple syrup

3 cups Garlic Chicken Stock (*see* page 107) or Vegetable Stock (224)

Pepper and nutmeg to taste

1 pinch red pepper flakes

½ cup heavy (35%) cream

This recipe comes from Chris and Melissa Velden of Flying Apron Cookery, a Nova Scotia business specializing in local and sustainable foods. I first became acquainted with them at the Lunenburg Farmers' Market, and have become hopelessly addicted to their products. I'm especially fond of their "Souper Mix," a mélange of finely minced, fresh vegetables and herbs that I use as a bouillon whenever I'm short of stock.

Combine butter, onion, and salt in a large saucepan over medium heat. Sauté until soft, about 5 minutes. Add the parsnips and garlic and sauté for 2 additional minutes. Add maple syrup and continue to cook, stirring, for another 2 minutes.

Add stock, pepper, nutmeg, and red pepper flakes. Bring to a simmer, and continue to simmer until parsnips are cooked through, about 15 minutes.

Puree with an immersion blender or transfer to a stand blender, puree, and return to pot. Add cream, warm over low heat, and serve.

Pears

Bosc, Anjou, Comice, Bartlett, Clapp—each varietal has its strengths, and the only way to get to know them is to try them all. Pears love cheese, so slice them on the side of a cheese plate for an appealing, no-cook presentation.

Pears keep well on the counter for up to 2 weeks, so there's no need to refrigerate them. To freeze pears, peel, core, quarter, combine with simple syrup (*see* Get Liquid With It, page 8) to cover in a saucepan, bring almost to a simmer over medium heat, remove from heat, add a teaspoon of lemon or rhubarb juice, pack, and freeze. To dehydrate, peel, slice, and dry for 6 to 20 hours.

In addition to these recipes, pears can also be used in place of apples in Cheddar Apple Pie (*see* page 20).

Pear Brie Salad

If you aren't a Brie fan, you may try this salad with another cheese—I also like it with pepper Boursin or a mild white cheddar.

Serves 2

- -

3 cups chopped crisp salad greens

1 pear, cored and thinly sliced

½ cup crumbled Brie

¼ cup crumbled pecans

3 tablespoons almond, hazelnut, or walnut oil

1 tablespoon lemon juice

2 tablespoons apple cider

¼ teaspoon salt

¼ teaspoon pepper

In a salad bowl, toss salad greens, pear slices, Brie, and pecans. In a second bowl, whisk oil, lemon juice, apple cider, salt, and pepper. Add dressing to salad, toss, and serve.

Pears Noisette

Serves 4

----

1 teaspoon vanilla
½ cup sugar, divided
1 egg white
⅔ cup crushed
    hazelnuts
3 large or 5 small,
    ripe pears (any
    varietal), peeled,
    cored, and halved
⅓ cup water

Candy-crisped pears—this recipe skips straight to the good stuff. Substitute crushed walnuts or pecans if you'd rather, or add a few tablespoons of your favourite liqueur to the roasting water for a more grown-up taste.

Position a rack in the middle of the oven and preheat to 350°F. Butter two large baking dishes and set aside.

Combine vanilla, ¼ cup of the sugar, and egg white in a mixing bowl and whisk. Add hazelnuts and stir. Pour mixture into one of the baking dishes and bake until golden, about 20 minutes. Cool on a rack.

Increase oven temperature to 400°F. Sprinkle remaining sugar on the bottom of the second baking dish and place pears, flat side down, on the sugared dish.

Roast for 30 minutes, then add water, stir, and roast another 20 minutes. Crumble hazelnut topping over roasted pears and serve warm.

Poached Pears

Serves 4

----

4 cups water
1¼ cups sugar
1 cinnamon stick
1 teaspoon whole
    cloves
4 large or 6 small,
    ripe pears, peeled,
    cored, and
    quartered

These pears are great on ice cream or with a few ginger cookies. Or both.

Combine water, sugar, cinnamon stick, and cloves in a saucepan. Heat on medium-low, stirring occasionally, until sugar dissolves, about 8 minutes.

Add quartered pears and cover. Simmer until pears are tender, about 20 minutes. Allow to cool in liquid for 20 minutes, and serve.

Pear Rosemary Cornbread

Serves 6

- -

2 cups cornmeal

½ cup all-purpose
flour

3 teaspoons baking
powder

1 teaspoon salt

2 tablespoons sugar

2 eggs

1½ cups milk

5 tablespoons butter,
melted

1 cup peeled, cored,
finely chopped
pear

2 teaspoons fresh
rosemary, finely
minced

Serve with a little crème fraîche or yogurt for an unforgettable breakfast. Or, for a more dessert-like cornbread, replace the rosemary with 2 tablespoons of sliced almonds and increase the sugar to ¼ cup.

Preheat oven to 400°F. Generously grease a 9-by-9-inch baking pan and set aside.

In a mixing bowl, combine cornmeal, flour, baking powder, salt, and sugar and whisk to combine.

In a second bowl, combine eggs, milk, and melted butter and whisk. Add dry ingredients, pear, and rosemary, and stir with a spoon until thoroughly blended.

Transfer batter to prepared baking pan and bake for 25 minutes. Serve cool or warm.

Peas

$\mathcal{E}$asy to grow and tempting to taste buds, peas love to please. Originally from the Middle East, peas are now grown in greater numbers in Canada than in any other country in the world. They're a favourite garden crop for children because they grow so quickly and can be eaten sweet, right of the vine.

Snap peas, snow peas, and pea pods all keep in the refrigerator in an open container for up to 5 days. To freeze, blanch shelled peas or pea pods for 2 minutes and pack plain or in stock. To dehydrate any kind of pea, dry for 5 to 14 hours.

Mint Pea Soup

Serves 4

- -

2 tablespoons extra-
    virgin olive oil
1 tablespoon lemon
    juice
2 cloves garlic,
    minced or pressed
4 cups peas
    (fresh, or frozen
    and thawed)
⅓ cup finely
    chopped fresh
    mint
6 cups Vegetable
    Stock (*see* page
    224)
¾ cup heavy (35%)
    cream
Salt and pepper
    to taste

Mint and pea are a classic combination. This soup has stood the test of time for good reason, as you can taste for yourself.

Combine olive oil, lemon juice, garlic, peas, and mint in a stockpot over medium heat. Sauté, stirring frequently, for 5 minutes.

Add stock and bring to a simmer. Simmer for 20 minutes. Puree with an immersion blender, or remove to a stand blender, puree, and return to pot.

Add cream, salt, and pepper, and heat on low until warmed through. Serve immediately.

Three Pea Stir-Fry

Serves 4

----

2 tablespoons peanut
oil
1 cup snow pea pods
(fresh, or frozen
and thawed)
1 cup shelled green
peas (fresh,
or frozen and
thawed)
1 cup trimmed,
chopped snap
peas (fresh,
or frozen and
thawed)
2 cloves garlic,
minced or pressed
1 tablespoon minced
ginger
1 tablespoon Sriracha
(or other hot
pepper sauce)
2 teaspoons soy
sauce

This is the dish for the true pea lover. Using three different kinds of popular garden peas adds depth and dimensionality to their green goodness.

Heat peanut oil in a sauté pan over medium-high heat, then add snow pea pods, green peas, snap peas, garlic, and ginger. Sauté, stirring, for 4 minutes.

Remove from heat, add hot pepper sauce and soy sauce, and stir to combine. Serve with rice.

Pea Hummus

Serves 4

- -

2 cups shelled peas
(fresh, dried
and rehydrated,
or frozen and
thawed)
½ cup minced
fresh cilantro
2 cloves garlic,
pressed or minced
1 teaspoon cumin
2 tablespoons peanut
butter
1 tablespoon sesame
oil
2 teaspoons lemon
juice
1 teaspoon plain salt

Traditional hummus is made from chickpeas. This green pea version has the same creamy, spiced quality that I love in hummus, complemented by a layer of garden freshness.

Bring a saucepan of salted water to a boil. Add peas and cook until just tender, about 8 minutes. Drain and cool peas.

Combine cooked peas and all other ingredients in a blender or food processor; puree. Serve immediately.

Dilly Peas

Serves 4

3 cups tender young
    peas (fresh,
    or frozen and
    thawed)
1 teaspoon Herb Salt
    (see page 120) or
    ½ teaspoon plain
    salt
½ cup crème fraîche
    or sour cream
2 tablespoons butter
1 tablespoon minced
    dill

If you grow a bit of dill indoors in the winter and keep some peas in the freezer, you can evoke a summer's day any time you need one in just about 10 minutes.

Bring a saucepan of salted water to a boil over medium heat. Add peas and cook, stirring occasionally, until peas are cooked through but still bright green, about 7 minutes. Drain and set aside.

Combine salt, crème fraîche or sour cream, and butter in a saucepan. Cook over medium-low heat until butter is melted. Add peas and dill and cook, stirring, 2 minutes more. Serve immediately.

Peppers

rowing peppers can be a challenge in the Maritimes, so we're all the more excited to enjoy the successes—be they spicy or mild varietals. If you get your peppers in a CSA box or at your local farmers' market, consider them a testament to the expertise of the growers you support.

Peppers can stay on a cool countertop for 2 to 3 days and in the crisper for up to 5. To freeze, seed and cut into pieces of desired size. Do not blanch. Freeze plain or in stock. I like to first roast peppers before freezing (following the first paragraph of the instructions for Pasta with Roasted Green Pepper Sauce, *see* page 169). To dehydrate, seed and cut into pieces of desired size, then dry for 5 to 12 hours.

In addition to the recipes below, peppers are used for Fresh Salsa (205) .

Jalapeño Mayonnaise

Yield: About ¾ cup

- -

¾ cup mayonnaise
1 fresh jalapeño
    (or other spicy
    pepper), stemmed,
    seeded, and
    minced
1–2 cloves garlic,
    minced or pressed
1½ teaspoons lime
    juice

This spicy mayo is my secret ingredient in the world's least boring grilled cheese sandwich—use instead of butter to "grease" the outside of the bread before pan-grilling. If you wish, you may add 2 tablespoons of minced, fresh cilantro for use in a sandwich or salad.

Combine all ingredients in a small bowl and whisk. Cover tightly and refrigerate for at least 2 hours before using. Jalapeño Mayonnaise will keep in the refrigerator for up to 5 days.

Fresh Red Pepper Sauce

**Yield: Approximately
2 cups**

- -

2 cups bite-sized
    pepper pieces
    (fresh, dried
    and rehydrated,
    or frozen and
    thawed)
½ teaspoon salt
2 tablespoons lime
    juice

Use this recipe to make a mild but flavourful sauce out of sweet peppers, a spicy condiment out of hot peppers, or a moderately spicy topping—using a blend of sweet and hot.

Combine all ingredients with just enough water to cover in a blender or food processor, and puree.

Transfer mixture to a saucepan and bring to a simmer over medium-low heat. Simmer for 10 minutes. Will keep in the refrigerator for 1 week or the freezer for 6 months.

Marinated Roasted Peppers

Yield: 3 pints

----

1 cup extra-virgin
  olive oil, divided
4 pounds seeded,
  fresh pepper slices
  (any varietal or
  combination)
1 cup lemon juice
2 cups white vinegar
3 cloves garlic,
  minced or pressed
1 tablespoon Herb
  Salt (*see* page 120)
  or 2 teaspoons
  plain salt

You can use this recipe for any kind of pepper—bell, jalapeño, or whatever else you've got. Serve them chopped up in pastas and casseroles, or as a snack on crackers with cheese.

Preheat broiler on oven and position a rack on the highest rung. Combine 1 tablespoon of the olive oil with pepper slices in a mixing bowl and toss until slices are coated.

Place oiled slices on a baking sheet, skin side up, and broil until skins blister and blacken, about 5 minutes. Remove from oven and transfer peppers to a bowl and cover. Set aside.

Combine remaining olive oil, lemon juice, vinegar, garlic, and salt in a sauce pan and bring to a boil over medium-high heat. Boil for 2 minutes then remove from heat.

When peppers are cool enough to handle, remove the blackened skins to the best of your ability (a little left behind is fine). Evenly distribute slices between 3 pint jars, then fill jars with liquid mixture, making sure that one garlic clove goes into each jar. Lid and refrigerate. Peppers will keep up to 2 months.

Stuffed Bell Peppers

Serves 4

----

6 large fresh bell
    peppers (any
    colour or a
    combination),
    divided
1 onion, minced
4 tablespoons extra-
    virgin olive oil
2 teaspoons Herb
    Salt (*see* page 120)
    or 1 teaspoon plain
    salt
1 pound cooked
    ground beef or
    lentils
1½ cup cooked rice
½ cup tomato paste
2 tablespoons
    Sriracha (or other
    hot pepper sauce)
1 tablespoon lemon
    juice

This recipe is best if you use contrasting-coloured peppers for your 4 whole and 2 minced peppers—so, for instance, you might stuff green peppers with chopped red peppers, or vice versa. It's a great way to use peppers in various stages of ripeness from your garden. If your homegrown peppers are as small as mine, you may wish to increase or even double the number of peppers in the recipe, while keeping the other ingredients constant.

Preheat oven to 350°F.

Cut the tops off of 4 of the peppers and remove the seeds and pith (white connective material). Stand seeded peppers in a baking dish with ¼ cup water in the bottom and set aside. Seed and finely chop the remaining 2 peppers.

Combine chopped peppers, onion, olive oil, and salt in a sauté pan and sauté on medium-low, stirring occasionally, until onion is soft, about 10 minutes. Remove from heat.

Add cooked beef or lentils, rice, tomato paste, hot pepper sauce, and lemon juice to vegetables and stir to combine. Stuff mixture into 4 whole peppers.

Bake for 1 hour. Serve hot.

Pasta with Roasted Green Pepper Sauce

Serves 4

3 tablespoons extra-
    virgin olive oil,
    divided
4 cups fresh pepper
    pieces slices
1 onion, finely
    chopped
2 teaspoons Herb
    Salt (*see page 120*)
    or 1 teaspoon plain
    salt
3 cloves garlic,
    pressed or minced
1 tablespoon dark
    miso
1½ cups white wine
5 cups cooked
    fettuccine (or
    other long-strand
    pasta)
¼ cup minced fresh
    parsley

This sauce has an almost-bitter quality that some people particularly love. The roasting process brings out the best of the flavour in the unripe peppers, making for a great dish to have in your back pocket when the nippy weather arrives and you're caught with loads of green peppers still perched on the plant.

Preheat broiler on oven and position a rack on the highest rung. Combine 1 tablespoon of the olive oil with pepper slices in a mixing bowl and toss until slices are coated.

Place oiled slices on a baking sheet, skin side up, and broil until skins blister and blacken, about 5 minutes. Remove from oven and transfer peppers to a bowl and cover. Set aside.

Combine remaining 2 tablespoons of olive oil, onion, and salt in a stockpot and sauté on medium-low, stirring occasionally, until onion is soft, about 10 minutes.

Add garlic and sauté for 1 minute more. Add miso and wine. Turn up heat to medium and simmer, stirring occasionally, for 5 minutes.

Rub and peel roasted pepper slices to remove charred skin. Add roasted peppers to mixture in stockpot. Puree with stick blender, or remove to stand blender, puree, and return to pot. Serve over cooked pasta and top with minced parsley.

Plums

Plums do very well in the Maritimes, and are available in an array of shapes, sizes, and tastes rivalled only by apples. I must admit that they're my favourite of the stone fruits. Plums can also be substituted for up to half the apples in Cheddar Apple Pie (*see* page 20).

To freeze plums, pit, halve, and freeze plain or in simple syrup (*see* Get Liquid With It, page 8). To dehydrate, pit, halve, and dry for 12 to 18 hours.

Plum Coulis

Yield:
approximately 1 cup

- -

3 large or 5 small
    plums, pitted and
    roughly chopped
    (fresh, dried
    and rehydrated,
    or frozen and
    thawed)
3 tablespoons water
Pepper to taste

This recipe is a good use for plums that aren't ripe or sweet enough for eating out of hand. It makes a tart, fruity sauce that is terrific on pork or chicken.

Combine all ingredients in the blender and pulse to puree. Pass puree through a fine sieve to remove solids. Serve, room temperature, as a dressing for meat or fish.

Plum Granita

Serves 6–8

- -

1 cup sugar
1½ cups water
1 tablespoon vanilla
2 teaspoons
    cinnamon
¼ teaspoon ground
    clove
3 pounds fresh ripe
    plums, pitted and
    roughly chopped

Serve this granita plain or layered with whipped cream and slices of fresh plum or other fruits on top for an elegant presentation. Granita will keep for up to 2 weeks.

Combine sugar, water, vanilla, cinnamon, and clove in a small saucepan. Bring to a simmer over medium heat and cook, stirring, for 5 minutes. Set syrup aside to cool.

Thoroughly puree chopped plums in a blender or food processor. Press through a fine sieve and discard solids. Add syrup to puree and pulse again until thoroughly combined.

Transfer mixture to a glass or plastic container and freeze for 4–6 hours, stirring thoroughly every 30 minutes, until well-frozen.

Plum Applesauce

Serves 6

- 2 pounds fresh apples (any varietal), peeled, cored, and roughly chopped
- 2 pounds fresh plums, peeled and pitted
- Sugar or honey to taste

Cooking time for this recipe varies widely by fruit varietal and degree of ripeness, and so does the amount of sweetener needed, according to those same variables as well as personal taste. This is a good, easy recipe for learning to cook without a recipe, which should be a long-term goal for any seasonal food lover. A wide span of varietals expands our enjoyment of life! Not one of them cooks up the same as another. If you're planning to serve this as baby food, don't add sweetener but be sure to use particularly ripe, naturally sweet fruit.

Combine all ingredients in a stockpot over medium-low heat.

Cook, covered, stirring occasionally until fruit is broken down, 1½ to 3 hours. Taste to adjust sweetness. Plum applesauce keeps for 1 week in the fridge and 1 year in the freezer.

Plum Brandy

Yield: About 2 cups

- 10 fresh plums, pitted and sliced
- 2 cups brandy
- ½ cup sugar

Traditionally known as *slivovitz* across Eastern Europe, plum brandy has been distilled in Bulgarian monasteries since the fourteenth century. Experiment with different plums or combinations to make your own local version.

Combine all ingredients in a clean glass container. Infuse in a dark, cool place for 1 month.

Strain through a piece of cheesecloth or a coffee filter. Reserve plums to serve on ice cream or to puree for alcoholic smoothies or ice pops.

Store liqueur in a clean, sealed bottle in the refrigerator, where it will keep indefinitely.

Potatoes

I love potatoes, and not just because I can fill up old clothes with potting soil and grow a cool potato scarecrow in them, but because they are one vegetable that even vegetable dislikers are guaranteed to eat. Nobody visits my home without being fed produce from the garden, and potatoes are a sure winner every time. Odds are it's the same for you. In addition to the recipes below, potatoes are also featured in Ginger Bean Potato Salad (*see* page 30).

Potatoes shouldn't be refrigerated. They keep best in a cool, dark, dry spot. There's little sense in freezing them, but they are a good candidate for dehydration. To dehydrate, peel if desired, slice, and dry for 6 to 12 hours until crisp.

The easiest way to make a potato is simply to bake it. Preheat the oven to 375°F, poke a few holes in a clean potato with a fork, and bake until tender, about 1 hour.

Enjoy a baked potato with topped with Bean and Roasted Tomato Stew (*see* page 31), Broccoli Jack Soup (52), Cauliflower Asiago Soup (73), Tomato Cauliflower Curry (76), Walnut Scape Pesto (104), Green Gumbo (112), Herb Butter (118), Herb Pesto (121), Frizzled Leeks (128), Jalapeño Mayonnaise (165), Fresh Red Pepper Sauce (165), Fresh Salsa (205), Sun-Dried Tomato Pesto (206), Fresh Tomato Sauce (207), or a combination.

Garlic-Roasted New Potatoes

Serves 6

- -

2 pounds new
potatoes, cleaned
and chopped into
bite-sized chunks

3 tablespoons extra-
virgin olive oil

4 cloves garlic, finely
minced

1 tablespoon
minced rosemary,
thyme, sage, or a
combination

1 teaspoon Herb Salt
(*see* page 120) or
1 teaspoon plain
salt

Dense, succulent new potatoes need little in the way of bells and whistles to make a memorable meal. I have been guilty of eating my fill of these while ignoring the meat on my plate.

Position a rack in the upper third of the oven and preheat to 425°F.

Combine all ingredients in a mixing bowl and toss. Spread potatoes out on a baking sheet.

Roast until browned and cooked through, about 45 minutes, stirring once.

Twice-Baked Potatoes

Serves 4

----

4 large potatoes
1 cup sour cream
1 cup grated cheese
1 cup cooked beans
    or chopped,
    cooked meat (any
    kind)
1 cup cooked
    vegetables (any
    kind)

Four baked potatoes and 4 cups of stuff: this recipe is a favourite way to re-imagine our leftovers. Possible combinations include cheddar, ham, and green beans; Parmesan, tuna, and tomato; or mozzarella, chicken sausage, and bell pepper.

Preheat oven to 400°F. Poke each potato several times with a fork to create steam vents. Place potatoes directly on the rack and bake for 75 minutes, then allow to cool for about 30 minutes.

Slice potatoes in half, lengthwise, and scoop out baked insides. Combine scooped-out potato, sour cream, cheese, meat or beans, and vegetables in a mixing bowl and blend thoroughly.

Fill potato skins with mixture and return to hot oven for another 40 minutes. Allow to cool for 10 minutes, then serve.

Curried Potato Soup

Serves 6–8

This soup includes about everything good in the garden plus curry to boot. A late-summer favourite.

4 tablespoons butter

2 small onions, finely chopped

2 teaspoons Herb Salt (*see* page 120) or 1 teaspoon plain salt

3 large carrots, peeled and sliced

2 pounds potatoes, peeled and chopped into bite-sized pieces

6 cups Garlic Chicken Stock (*see* page 107) or Vegetable Stock (224)

2 tablespoons curry powder

2 large or 3 small tomatoes, diced

2 zucchini (or other summer squash), chopped into bite-sized pieces

½ cup minced cilantro

Combine butter, onion, and salt in a stockpot over medium heat. Sauté, stirring occasionally, until onion begins to brown, about 5 minutes.

Add carrots, potatoes, stock, and curry powder. Simmer, uncovered, for 30 minutes. Add tomatoes and squash and cook for another 10 minutes or until all vegetables are cooked through.

Using an immersion blender, puree about half of the soup, leaving the other half chunky. Alternatively, remove half of the soup to a stand blender, puree, and return to soup pot. Serve garnished with minced cilantro.

Main Dish Mashed Potatoes

Serves 4

----

2 pounds potatoes,
   peeled and
   roughly chopped
3 cups Garlic Chicken
   Stock (*see* page
   107) or Vegetable
   Stock (224)
2 cloves garlic,
   peeled and
   roughly chopped
2 tablespoons butter
⅓ cup heavy (35%)
   cream
¼ cup Boursin (or
   similar soft cheese)

The stock cooked into these mashed potatoes, along with the protein-rich cheese, qualifies it as a nutritional powerhouse. Add cooked, chopped vegetables or meat to taste.

Combine potatoes, stock, and garlic in a stockpot and bring to a boil over medium-high heat.

Boil, uncovered, stirring frequently, until potatoes are mostly soft. Reduce heat to medium-low.

Using a potato masher or fork, mash softened potatoes and garlic into the stock and continue to cook until potatoes have a mashed-potato consistency.

Add butter, cream, and cheese and mash to combine. Remove from heat and serve immediately.

Ham and Potato Hash

Serves 4

----

6 small, 3 medium, or
    2 large potatoes,
    peeled and
    chopped into bite-
    sized cubes
3 tablespoons butter
1 teaspoon Herb Salt
    (*see* page 120)
    or ½ teaspoon
    regular salt
1 onion, minced
1 cup ham, chopped
    into bite-sized
    cubes
Pepper to taste
Optional add-ins:
    1 cup chopped
    tomato;
    1 chopped bell
    pepper (or other
    mild pepper);
    1 minced hot
    pepper;
    1 tablespoon fresh
    thyme, parsley, or
    cilantro, packed
    and minced;
    ½ teaspoon dried
    thyme, parsley, or
    cilantro;
    1 tablespoon hot
    pepper sauce

This classic hash is a family-pleaser for breakfast, lunch, or dinner. Put a few bowls of the suggested add-ins on the side and let everyone create a personalized dish.

Bring a large pan of water to a simmer over medium heat and add chopped potatoes. Simmer, stirring occasionally, for 10 minutes, or until mostly cooked but still firm.

In the meantime, melt butter in a skillet over medium heat. Add salt and minced onion and sauté, stirring occasionally, until onion is soft and fragrant, about 10 minutes.

Add cooked potatoes and all other remaining ingredients, including any optional add-ins. Cook until browned to taste, about 10 minutes.

Radishes

With a long season and a maturity period of only 3 weeks, radishes are a great starter vegetable for the new or young gardener. The strong, rich pinks and purples of many varietals tempt even the pickiest palate. They are excellent raw, either out of hand or sliced into salads.

Radishes keep best if you separate the greens from the roots right away. Wash and keep the roots in an open container but covered with a damp towel. Stored this way, they will keep well for up to 1 week. Radish greens may be eaten raw in salads or cooked like any other hearty green.

Radishes should not be frozen raw, but they do freeze well cooked. Pack cooked, plain, or in stock. Dry by slicing and dehydrating at 130°F for 5 to 12 hours.

Radish and Carrot Slaw

Serves 6

- - - - - - - - - - - - - - - - - - -

1 tablespoon Sriracha
(or other hot
pepper sauce)
¼ cup lemon juice
¾ cup minced fresh
parsley
1 teaspoon salt
⅔ cup extra-virgin
olive oil
4 large fresh carrots,
peeled and
shredded
2 cups (2–4 bunches,
depending on size
& season) peeled,
shredded fresh
radishes

If your familiarity with slaws begins and ends with coleslaw, this dish might seem a little unusual—but give it a chance; it's a crowd-pleaser, especially at a picnic or barbeque.

Combine hot sauce, lemon juice, parsley, salt, and olive oil in a blender or food processor and puree.

Combine vinaigrette, shredded carrots, and shredded radishes in a serving bowl and toss. Cover and refrigerate for at least 15 minutes, toss again, and serve.

Pan-Fried Radishes

Serves 4

- - - - - - - - - - - - - - - - - - -

2 tablespoons butter
2 cups (2–4 bunches,
depending on
size & season)
clean, diced fresh
radishes
¼ cup diced fresh
chives
Salt and pepper to
taste

This simple radish preparation makes a good side dish or can be layered on top of lettuce for a warm salad.

Heat butter in a sauté pan over medium heat. Add diced radishes and cook, stirring frequently, until lightly browned, about 4 minutes.

Add chives, salt, and pepper and cook, stirring for 1 minute more. Serve immediately.

Radish Risotto

This Italian dish is a sophisticated way to welcome the spring.

6 tablespoons butter,
divided

1 onion, minced

2 teaspoons Herb
Salt (*see* page 120)
or 1 teaspoon plain
salt

2 cloves garlic,
minced or pressed

1 pound arborio rice

½ cup white wine

8 cups chicken stock
or Vegetable Stock
(*see* page 224)

1 pound fresh
radishes, cleaned,
trimmed, and
diced

1 tablespoon lemon
juice

1 tablespoon extra-
virgin olive oil

¾ cup grated
Parmesan

Pepper to taste

Combine 3 tablespoons of the butter, the onion, and the salt in a sauté pan and sauté on medium-low, stirring occasionally, until onion is soft, about 10 minutes.

Add garlic and rice and sauté an additional 2 minutes, stirring.

Turn heat to medium and add wine and cook, stirring, another 2 minutes. Add stock, 1 cup at a time, as rice absorbs the liquid, stirring often.

In the meantime, combine radishes, lemon juice, and olive oil in a mixing bowl and toss. Once rice has absorbed all liquid, add Parmesan and remaining 3 tablespoons of butter.

Remove from heat and add pepper to taste. Serve topped with radish mixture.

Rhubarb

One of my fondest childhood memories is of meeting my best friend Andy, who lived three houses down, and picking rhubarb from the yard of the neighbour exactly in between our homes. We would knock on her back door, show her our harvest, and she would bring us a dish of sugar. We would sit on the porch and dip the stalks into the sugar, enjoying nature's Lik-A-Stick. Today, rhubarb is a household favourite that we rediscover every spring before other plants have even poked their heads up. Plant it once and you'll have it forever!

Rhubarb keeps best in an open container in the crisper with a damp towel. It will keep this way for 4 to 5 days. To freeze, cut into bite-sized pieces, blanch for 1 minute, and freeze plain or in simple syrup (*see* Get Liquid With It, page 8). Dry rhubarb by dehydrating at 130°F for 6 to 14 hours.

Caramelized Rhubarb Jam

Yield: About 1 litre

- -

4 cups chopped fresh
   rhubarb

1 teaspoon vanilla
   extract

2½ cups sugar
   (roughly; adjust to
   taste)

Based on the recipe from Jess Thomson's blog, *Hogwash*, this jam is a simple, enticingly caramel-ish alternative to the standard compote, and a great way to get jamming early in the season.

Place a rack in the upper-third of the oven and preheat oven 375°F. Combine all ingredients in a large, shallow baking pan.

Roast rhubarb, stirring only once, for 3 to 4 hours or until stalk fibres are broken down and surface has a brown, caramelized appearance.

If canning with sterilized equipment, can immediately; otherwise, set aside for 30 minutes to cool, then transfer to containers and refrigerate or freeze until use. Jam will keep up to 1 month in the refrigerator or 6 months in the freezer.

Rhubarb All (Spice) Stars

Serves 8

- -

2¼ cups pastry flour

¼ cup brown sugar

1 cup cold butter, cut
   into small pieces

½ cup cold milk

3 cups chopped fresh
   rhubarb

1 egg

1½ cups white sugar

1½ teaspoons
   ground allspice

1 cup sour cream

⅓ cup all-purpose
   flour

As an alternative to making a regular-sized pie, you may use half a dozen short canning jars to make individual-sized pies, using one dough-star per pie, and shortening baking time to about 35 minutes.

Combine pastry flour, brown sugar, butter, and milk in a mixing bowl until just integrated. Wrap in plastic wrap and refrigerate for at least 1 hour, and as long as overnight.

Preheat oven to 450°F.

Roll pie dough out on a lightly floured surface with a floured rolling pin. Using a star-shaped cookie cutter, cut out 5–7 stars and set aside. Press remaining pie dough evenly into a pie pan and form an even edge around the top with your fingertips. Evenly distribute sliced rhubarb in the pan.

Mix all remaining ingredients with a whisk or a fork until fully integrated to create custard. Pour custard over rhubarb. Mixture should come to just below the rim of the pie. Place dough-stars lightly on top of custard, distributing them evenly across surface of the pie.

Place pie on a cookie sheet and bake for 20 minutes. Turn heat down to 350°F; bake until filling is slightly jiggly and topping is golden brown, about 50 minutes. Let cool completely on rack before eating.

Slow-Roast Rhubarb Chicken

Serves 6–8

4½ cups diced
    rhubarb, divided
    (fresh, dried
    and rehydrated,
    or frozen and
    thawed)
Zest of 1 lemon
1 bay leaf
2 tablespoons salt,
    divided
1 whole chicken
Juice of 1 lemon
¼ cup extra-virgin
    olive oil
¼ cup dark rum

Rhubarb's bright, acidic tones combine with dark spiced rum to scent the flesh of this roast chicken with an irresistible mélange, while slow-roasting makes for a particularly tender and flavourful meat.

Preheat oven to 400°F, and butter a roasting pan. Combine diced rhubarb, lemon zest, bay leaf, and 1 tablespoon of the salt in a mixing bowl and set aside.

Wash and rinse chicken, then gently pat dry and place in roasting pan. Stuff chicken with rhubarb mixture.

Combine remaining tablespoon of salt, lemon juice, olive oil, and rum in a second mixing bowl. Drizzle mixture evenly over chicken.

Bake for 20 minutes, then reduce heat to 275°F. Baste chicken with liquid in the roasting pan.

Continue to bake, basting once an hour, until a meat thermometer plunged into the thickest part of the breast has reached 160°F, about 3 to 5 hours (depending on the size of the chicken). Remove from oven, allow meat to rest for 30 minutes, carve, and serve.

Rhubarb Gin

Yield: 750 millilitres

----

2 cups chopped fresh
    rhubarb
750 millilitres gin

Rhubarb, with its acidic bite, has a wonderful affinity for the juniper berries and coriander seed that flavour gin. This marriage of flavours is the perfect palate-pleaser.

Combine gin and rhubarb in a pitcher. Cover well with plastic wrap and store in refrigerator for 1 week. Strain out rhubarb and return gin to a clean bottle. Enjoy anytime with tonic water or in cocktails. Gin will keep for 3 to 4 months in the refrigerator.

Summer Squash

Summer squash is a subset of squash that is harvested while still immature and tender, and includes zucchini, pattypan squash, yellow squash, and crookneck squash. They are notorious for jumping out at you in big bushels just when you thought you had a handle on your garden. When I was a girl, a farmer friend of the family used to leave grocery bags of zucchini on our doorstep, ring the bell, and drive away like a bat out of hell. (And I'm talking about those big, old-fashioned paper bags, not these suspicious little plastic bags they use nowadays.)

Luckily, summer squash are versatile and easy to preserve. My favourite simple preparation is to steam them and serve with butter, salt, and pepper. Zucchini and other summer squash can be stored on a cool counter for 3 to 4 days, or for up to 1 week in the refrigerator. To freeze summer squash, blanch bite-sized pieces for 3 minutes and pack plain or in stock. To dry, simply slice and dehydrate for 5 to 10 hours.

In addition to the recipes in this section, summer squash are featured in Curried Potato Soup (see page 178) and Cold Tomato Vegetable Soup (208).

Alice's Cheesecake

Serves 4

- -

1 onion, minced

3 tablespoons butter
   or extra-virgin
   olive oil, divided

2 teaspoons Herb
   Salt (*see* page 120)
   or 1 teaspoon plain
   salt

3 cups cracker
   crumbs

1 tablespoon lemon
   juice

2 cups ricotta cheese

1 cup grated
   Parmesan

2 teaspoons smoked
   paprika

2 large eggs

2 large zucchini,
   grated (fresh, dried
   and rehydrated,
   or frozen and
   thawed)

Cheese lovers, this one is for you. Easy enough to throw together at the end of a workday, this vegetarian entrée is also elegant enough to impress a last-minute guest.

Preheat the oven to 350°F. Generously grease a pie pan.

Combine onion, half the butter or olive oil, and salt in a sauté pan and sauté on medium-low, stirring occasionally, until onion is soft, about 10 minutes.

Combine the cracker crumbs, lemon juice, and remaining butter or olive oil in a mixing bowl and toss. Transfer mixture to a baking sheet and toast in the oven, stirring occasionally, for 20 minutes. Distribute toasted cracker crumbs evenly on bottom of pie pan.

In a second mixing bowl, combine ricotta, Parmesan, paprika, and eggs and beat until thoroughly combined. Add grated zucchini and onion mixture and stir to combine. Gently distribute mixture evenly on top of bread crumbs.

Bake for 1 hour. Cool to room temperature, top with fresh chopped herbs if desired, and serve.

Zucchini Pickles

Yield: approximately 4 pints

- -

1 pound (about
4 small) fresh
zucchini (or other
summer squash),
sliced into thin sticks

1 large onion, finely
    minced

2 cloves garlic,
    chopped

3 tablespoons Herb
    Salt (*see page 120*)
    or 1½ tablespoons
    plain salt

¾ cup lemon juice

¾ cup white vinegar

1 fresh jalapeño
    pepper, roughly
    chopped

⅓ cup honey

A proven favourite among pickle lovers. Spicy and sweet, these vinegar-soaked spears jump up and grab you by the tongue. Keep in mind that these pickles are not sterile, so they should be stored in the refrigerator and consumed within 6 weeks.

Combine all ingredients in a mixing bowl and stir vigorously.

Transfer to glass jar, cover, and store in refrigerator for at least 1 week before consuming. Will keep in refrigerator for up to 6 weeks.

Garlic-Roasted Zucchini

Serves 4

----

1 pound zucchini,
cut into bite-
sized chunks,
about 3½ cups
(fresh, dried
and rehydrated,
or frozen and
thawed)
2 cloves garlic,
minced or pressed
¼ cup extra-virgin
olive oil
1 tablespoon minced
fresh dill, thyme,
or parsley
Salt and pepper to
taste

Simple and flavourful, this dish can be served by itself with almost any entrée. Puree any leftovers with stock and cream for an unforgettable soup the next day!

Position a rack in the upper-third of the oven and preheat to 450°F.

Combine all ingredients in a mixing bowl and toss. Transfer to a baking dish and bake until zucchini begins to brown, about 10 minutes. Serve hot.

Stuffed Squash

Serves 4

- -

This is a good recipe for using those larger zucchini and summer squash that you may have let linger in the garden a little too long.

4 fresh large zucchini (or other summer squash), each about 1 foot long

2 tablespoons extra-virgin olive oil

1 small onion, finely chopped

3 teaspoons Herb Salt (*see* page 120) or 1½ teaspoons plain salt

3 large tomatoes, diced

1 pound cooked sausage (any kind; turkey and vegetarian both work well)

¼ cup minced fresh herbs

1 large egg, beaten

2 teaspoons pepper

¾ cup shredded cheddar or Asiago cheese

Preheat oven to 375°F and fill a baking pan with ¼ inch of water and set aside.

Slice squash in half, lengthwise. Scrape out seedy insides with a spoon, leaving at least half the flesh, but making adequate space for stuffing.

Heat the olive oil in a sauté pan over medium heat. Add chopped onion and salt and cook, stirring occasionally, until onions are soft and golden, about 10 minutes. Remove from heat.

Add diced tomatoes, cooked sausage, minced herbs, beaten egg, and pepper to sautéed onions and stir to combine. Spoon mixture into hollowed-out squash, dividing it evenly. Sprinkle cheese on top.

Bake for about 45 minutes or until cheese is golden-brown. Serve hot.

Summer Squash Salad

Serves 4

----

4 small fresh zucchini
  (or other summer
  squash), thinly
  sliced
¼ cup minced basil
¼ cup crumbled
  pecans
¼ cup shredded
  Parmesan
3 tablespoons extra-
  virgin olive oil
1 tablespoon apple
  cider vinegar
Salt and pepper to
  taste

A quick salad to throw together, this zucchini recipe blends a variety of tastes with great success. It's just the right thing when you're sick of zucchini but determined not to waste the squash still sitting on your counter.

In a salad bowl, toss zucchini, basil, pecans, and Parmesan.

In a separate bowl, whisk olive oil and apple cider vinegar together and pour over salad.

Add salt and pepper, toss again, and serve immediately.

Tomatoes

A fresh, ripe, heirloom tomato from the Maritimes makes its grocery store counterpart look and taste like a red Styrofoam ball. Their variety is stupendous. If you wish to grow your own, you can choose virtually any size—from ball bearing to softball—in yellow, green, red, purple, or my new favourite, Berkeley Tie-Dye (available from Annapolis Seeds).

Don't ever refrigerate a tomato—it diminishes their flavour greatly. They will keep on the counter for up to 2 weeks. Influence their ripening by putting them in a paper bag with ripe apples. To freeze tomatoes, either blanch for 4 minutes, remove skins, and freeze whole; or cook first, by roasting or stewing, and then freeze. To dry, slice and dehydrate at 130°F for 12 to 24 hours. You may also dry tomatoes whole to make tomato "raisins" for pasta dishes, salads, and snacking. Because tomatoes have such a high water content, they take a particularly long time to dehydrate—but the results are worth it. Properly dried tomatoes keep indefinitely, but I strongly recommend storing yours in the freezer just to be on the safe side. If you store yours elsewhere, inspect for any sign of mould or "off" odour before use.

In addition to the recipes in this section, tomatoes are used in Bean and Roasted Tomato Stew (see page 31), Tomato Cauliflower Curry (76), Greens Frittata (114), Curried Potato Soup (178), and Stuffed Squash (197).

Roasted Tomato Soup

Serves 4

----

8 large fresh
   tomatoes (any
   varietal or a
   combination),
   chopped into bite-
   sized pieces
1 large onion, roughly
   chopped
6 whole cloves garlic,
   peeled
¼ cup minced basil
   or rosemary
2 teaspoons Herb
   Salt (*see* page 120)
   or 1 teaspoon plain
   salt
3 cups Vegetable
   Stock (*see* page
   224)
¼ cup minced
   parsley

Made with Vegetable Stock, this light soup is also vegan. It's a good choice for a potluck, or guests who may have food restrictions you don't know about. I love dishes that are a safe bet for everyone!

Preheat the oven to 375°F and position two racks in the middle of the oven. Oil two baking sheets.

Arrange chopped tomatoes, onions, garlic, and herbs on baking sheets and sprinkle evenly with salt. Bake until tomatoes are softened and onions begin to brown, about 45 minutes.

Combine vegetables and stock in a blender and puree until some small chunks remain. Garnish with parsley and serve.

Fresh Tomatoes with Basil and Mozzarella

Serves 4

----

1 pound ripe fresh
    tomatoes, sliced
1 tablespoon
    balsamic vinegar
1 tablespoon extra-
    virgin olive oil
1 cup whole basil
    leaves, loosely
    packed
¼ pound mozzarella,
    thinly sliced
Salt and pepper to
    taste

This is my favourite recipe for showcasing the heirloom tomatoes in my own garden and from my farmers' market. Both the basil and the mozzarella serve to accentuate the flavours of the tomato. A great way to show off your garden to guests!

Lay tomato slices on a serving plate. In a mixing bowl, whisk balsamic vinegar and oil together, then drizzle mixture over tomatoes.

Layer basil and mozzarella over tomato slices, and add salt and pepper to taste. Serve immediately.

Flavoured Dried Tomatoes

Yield: approximately 2 cups

- -

½ cup extra-virgin
  olive oil

¼ cup balsamic
  vinegar

2 cloves garlic,
  minced or pressed

¼ cup minced
  parsley, basil,
  oregano, thyme,
  marjoram, or a
  combination

3–4 pounds fresh
  tomatoes, sliced

Rehydrate these in stock to make a quick and intensely flavourful sauce.

Combine olive oil, vinegar, garlic, and herbs in a mixing bowl and whisk to combine. Add tomatoes and cover. Marinate in the refrigerator for 2 hours.

Preheat oven to 180°F. Place tomato slices on a baking sheet and dry in oven until mostly dry but still pliant (12–16 hours). Cool and store in freezer bags until ready to use.

Fresh Salsa

- - - - - - - - - - - - - - - - - - - -

1 small onion, finely
  chopped
4 cloves garlic,
  minced or pressed
2 fresh jalapeño
  peppers, finely
  chopped
¼ cup minced fresh
  cilantro
2 tablespoons lime
  juice
4 medium fresh
  tomatoes,
  chopped
1 heaping teaspoon
  salt

Considering the taste of the results, this recipe is deceptively easy. Bring it to a party and wait for them to ask, "Where did you get this incredible salsa?" before you tell them it's homemade. It's fun being considered a culinary rock star, you'll see.

Combine all ingredients in a mixing bowl and toss to combine.

Refrigerate for at least 2 hours to allow flavours to blend. Salsa will keep for 2 to 3 days in the refrigerator.

Sun-Dried Tomato Pesto

**Yield: approximately
6 cups**

- -

2 cups finely
　chopped dried
　tomatoes
2 cups grated
　Parmesan cheese
½ cup extra-virgin
　olive oil
½ cup tomato paste
1 cup minced fresh
　basil
Juice of 1 lime
Zest of 1 lime
4 cloves garlic,
　pressed or minced
Salt and pepper to
　taste

The pesto in this recipe is smooth and paste-like if made in a food processor, much like traditional pesto, but I prefer the slightly chunkier texture of the blender version. The better the quality of the tomatoes you dry, the better the pesto. I like to use a combination of varietals in different colours. Sometimes I add a couple of tablespoons of hot pepper sauce to warm it up even more. One recipe is enough to dress 3–4 easy meals of pasta, meat, or fish.

Combine all ingredients in a food processor or blender and pulse until it consists of fine, evenly mixed particles. Keeps in the refrigerator for 2 weeks, or the freezer for 6 months.

Fresh Tomato Sauce

Serves 4

- -

3 cups chopped fresh
  tomatoes
2 sticks fresh celery,
  diced
1 small onion, diced
2 fresh carrots,
  peeled and diced
1 tablespoon Herb
  Salt (*see* page 120)
  or 2 teaspoons
  plain salt
⅓ cup butter

The butter makes the difference in this sauce. To be frank, the more butter, the better; add even more than listed here if you like.

Combine all ingredients in a stockpot and bring to a simmer over medium-low heat. Continue to simmer, stirring occasionally, for 1 hour.

Puree with a stick blender or remove to a stand blender to puree. Serve with pasta as an entrée.

Cold Tomato Vegetable Soup

Serves 6

8 large fresh
  tomatoes, seeded
  and chopped
3 cups fresh tomato
  juice
3 fresh zucchini (or
  other summer
  squash), peeled
  and finely
  chopped
2 cloves garlic,
  minced
¼ cup minced,
  packed, fresh
  parsley
2 teaspoons Herb
  Salt (see page 120)
  or 1 teaspoon plain
  salt
2 cups Vegetable
  Stock (see page
  224)
1 tablespoon hot
  pepper sauce
2 tablespoons lemon
  juice
2 tablespoons extra-
  virgin olive oil
¼ cup minced,
  packed, fresh basil
1 teaspoon pepper
Kernels from 3 ears
  of fresh corn

This recipe is a delightful way to enjoy summer produce without any actual cooking. To create the tomato juice for this recipe, simply crush fresh tomatoes and strain juice out through a sieve, discarding solids. Between the juicing tomatoes and the chopped tomatoes, you will need a total of 12–15 fresh tomatoes.

Combine all ingredients in a storage container and stir.

Refrigerate for 12 to 24 hours. Serve cold.

Turnips and Rutabagas

The turnip is a small, white root vegetable that has been cultivated since antiquity, although to confuse matters, what's called a rutabaga in London is called a turnip in Scotland and many other locales, and where rutabagas are turnips, turnips are "Swedes." Turnips are also called "neeps," as in the "neeps and tatties" (potatoes) of a Burns supper. Before the pumpkin made it big, the turnip was a favoured vegetable for Halloween carving in Scotland and the North of England.

A rutabaga is a cross between a turnip and a cabbage. It far more resembles a turnip than a cabbage both structurally and in taste, and for culinary purposes they are interchangeable. For that matter, you can substitute kohlrabi (German turnip) for either. Baby turnips can be eaten raw in salads, just like radishes. As with beets, the greens of the turnip can be eaten when young and tender.

Rutabagas and turnips keep best in a closed container in the crisper, lightly covered with a damp towel. I do not recommend freezing rutabagas and turnips. To dehydrate either, peel, slice, and dry at 130°F for 12 to 16 hours.

Mashed Turnips

Serves 4

This is a good recipe for those older, drier turnips toward the end of season.

2 pounds turnip,
  peeled and
  chopped into bite-
  sized chunks
1 tablespoon Herb
  Salt (*see* page 120)
  or 2 teaspoons
  plain salt
½ cup heavy (35%)
  cream
1 tablespoon minced
  rosemary
2 tablespoons butter
Pepper to taste

Bring a large saucepan of salted water to a boil over medium-high water.

Add chopped turnips and salt and boil until tender, about 15 minutes Drain, then return turnips to the pot over low heat

Add cream, rosemary, butter, and pepper and mash turnips with a fork or masher. Serve immediately.

Rutabaga Bacon Roast

Serves 4

----

1 large rutabaga,
   peeled and cut
   into bite-sized
   chunks
4 slices bacon,
   chopped
1 onion, chopped
2 teaspoons Herb
   Salt (*see* page 120)
   or 1 teaspoon plain
   salt

This is a heavier vegetable dish. It works well as one of two or three vegetable dishes or to complement a light main, such as haddock. It's also excellent for people who "don't like vegetables," as those same folks inevitably love bacon.

Preheat oven to 400°F.

Toss all ingredients in a baking pan. Roast until bacon is crisped and vegetables are cooked through, about 45 minutes, tossing every 10 minutes to distribute bacon grease. Allow to cool for 5 minutes, then serve.

Scalloped Turnips

Serves 4

----

1 medium onion,
    peeled and thinly
    sliced
4 tablespoons butter
2 teaspoons Herb
    Salt (*see* page 120)
    or 1 teaspoon plain
    salt
6 large turnips,
    peeled and thinly
    sliced
Pepper to taste
1 cup heavy (35%)
    cream
¼ cup grated
    Parmesan

This is an appetizing alternative to scalloped potatoes. It goes nicely with a ham or meatloaf.

Preheat onion to 350°F. Butter a large baking dish and set aside.

Combine onion, butter, and salt in a sauté pan and sauté on medium-low, stirring occasionally, until onion is soft, about 10 minutes.

Layer turnips in the baking dish, sprinkling some of the sautéed onions and a grind of pepper between each layer. Pour cream over the entire dish after all turnip slices are laid down. Scatter grated Parmesan on the top layer.

Bake for 1 hour or until liquid is bubbling and turnips are fork-tender. Allow to cool for 10 minutes and serve.

Winter Squash

Pumpkins, acorn squash, Red Kuri, spaghetti squash, butternut, buttercup...winter squash are just so satisfying. You can wrangle several meals out of a single vegetable—who doesn't love that?

Technically, these North American natives are fruit, and lend themselves to sweet preparations very well. The simplest preparation for any winter squash is to cut it in big hunks, de-seed, and bake at 350°F for about 1 hour. Top with butter and brown sugar, maple syrup, or salt and pepper.

Winter squash shouldn't be refrigerated. They can keep up to several months in a cool, dark, dry place with good air circulation. To freeze winter squash, first cook by steaming or baking, then pack plain or with a small amount of stock added. I don't recommend dehydrating winter squash. Considering how well they keep without special preparation, there's not much point in going overboard, anyway.

Green Curry Pumpkin Soup

Serves 6–8

- 3 tablespoons peanut oil
- 1 large pumpkin (or 2 smaller winter squash), sliced into quarters and seeded
- 1 teaspoon salt
- 1 can coconut milk
- 5 cups chicken stock or Vegetable Stock (*see* page 224)
- 1 tablespoon green curry paste
- ½ cup finely chopped cilantro

This recipe is a slightly westernized version of an Asian classic. It pairs particularly well with an after-holiday turkey sandwich.

Position a rack in the centre of the oven and preheat to 375°F.

Slather peanut oil over pumpkin quarters and sprinkle with salt. Roast on a baking sheet for about 75 minutes, or until flesh is tender. Remove from oven and cool for 20 minutes.

Scoop flesh from squash into a stockpot. Add coconut milk, stock, and green curry paste and bring to a simmer over medium-low heat.

Puree with an immersion blender, or remove to a stand blender, puree, return to the pot, and bring back to a simmer. Serve with cilantro sprinkled on top.

Maple Squash Muffins

Yield: 12 muffins

- -

1½ cups all-purpose
    flour
½ teaspoon salt
1 teaspoon baking
    soda
1 teaspoon cinnamon
½ teaspoon allspice
1½ cups baked
    squash (fresh,
    or frozen and
    thawed)
⅓ cup melted butter
    or vegetable oil
1 teaspoon vanilla
2 eggs
⅔ cup maple syrup

This recipe is a good use of leftover squash from a meal—bake these muffins after a squash-centric dinner and eat them for breakfast the next day.

Preheat oven to 350°F and either grease a muffin pan or place liners in the cups.

Combine flour, salt, baking soda, cinnamon, and allspice in a mixing bowl and whisk thoroughly.

In a second mixing bowl, beat baked squash, butter or vegetable oil, vanilla, eggs, and maple syrup together.

Add dry ingredients to wet ingredients and stir until thoroughly combined. Pour batter into tin, filling each cup about ⅔ full.

Bake until a knife inserted in the middle comes out clean, about 20 minutes.

Top with cinnamon sugar if desired. Goes nicely with a little whipped cream or crème fraîche. Cool on a rack and serve warm or cool.

Almond Squash

Serves 4

----

4 cups peeled,
    seeded, bite-
    sized chunks of
    winter squash (any
    varietal)
1 teaspoon vanilla
    extract
¼ cup butter, melted
1 teaspoon salt
1 tablespoon lemon
    juice
1 cup sliced almonds

I like this recipe with the nut-friendly Red Kuri squash, known as *potimarron* in French—so-called because of the rich chestnut flavour of its flesh.

Preheat oven to 400°F.

Toss squash, vanilla, melted butter, salt, and lemon juice in a large baking pan and roast for 20 minutes. Sprinkle sliced almonds on top and roast another 8 minutes. Cool for 5 minutes and serve.

Pumpkin Ravioli

Serves 4

1½ cups cooked
    pumpkin puree
    (fresh, or frozen
    and thawed)
⅔ cup cream cheese
Zest of 1 lemon
½ teaspoon plain salt
¼ teaspoon pepper
1 egg
36 won ton wrappers

This dish is simple yet elegant. If you want to get fancy with it, peel extra curly, thin ribbons of lemon zest to scatter around the borders of the serving plate.

Combine pumpkin puree, cream cheese, lemon zest, salt, and pepper in a mixing bowl.

In a second bowl, lightly beat egg. Brush beaten egg over won ton wrappers. Place a spoonful of filling in each wrapper, fold wrapper over, and press edges together to seal.

Bring a large pot of salted water to a boil over medium-high heat. Boil ravioli until tender, about 3 minutes. Serve with butter and Parmesan or a cream sauce.

Chocolate Pumpkin Pie

**Yield: 2 pies,
8 servings each**

- -

Serve this pie warm with chocolate whipped cream for a little extra bang. It's also very nice with Red Kuri squash.

2¼ cups pastry flour
(all-purpose will
do in a pinch)
½ cup grated dark
chocolate
1 cup cold butter, cut
into small pieces
½ cup cold milk
3 cups cooked
(baked or
steamed) pumpkin
(or other winter
squash)
1 can (370 mL)
sweetened
condensed milk
2 teaspoons
cinnamon
2 teaspoons allspice
1 teaspoon vanilla
½ teaspoon salt
4 eggs

Combine flour, chocolate, butter, and milk in a mixing bowl or food processor. Cut together until dough just holds together. Wrap ball of dough in plastic. Chill wrapped ball in the refrigerator.

Combine cooked pumpkin, sweetened condensed milk, cinnamon, allspice, vanilla, salt, and eggs in a mixing bowl and beat together to form filling.

Preheat oven to 375°F. Remove dough from refrigerator. Divide into 2 parts and roll into large rounds. Arrange each in the bottom of a 9-inch pie plate. Divide filling between pies.

Bake until crust is browned and filling is set, about 1 hour. Cool on a rack and serve warm or cool.

Assorted Produce

E very local, seasonal food lover needs a few tricks in his or her back pocket for using a flexible range of produce—dishes that can be made with what's on hand at any given time. The following recipes make the most of fresh and dried produce to help you maximize whatever you've got, whenever you've got it.

Mixed-Fruit Compote

**Yield: approximately
1 quart**

- -

3 cups mixed dried
    fruit
2 cups apple cider
Sugar to taste
1 teaspoon cinnamon
    (optional)

Use this compote as pie filling, oatmeal topping, or straight up as a warm or cold side dish or snack.

Combine all ingredients in a saucepan on the stove and bring to a simmer over medium-low heat. Simmer, stirring occasionally, for 20 minutes.

Remove from heat and use or serve warm or store, covered, in the refrigerator for up to 1 week.

Re-Veggie Soup

Serves 4

----

6 cups Garlic Chicken
    Stock (*see* page
    107) or Vegetable
    Stock (224)
3 cups diced, dried
    mixed vegetables
1 cup diced, cooked
    meat
Herb Salt (*see* page
    120) or plain salt to
    taste
Pepper to taste

This is a quick, easy, nutritious, and delicious meal any time of year. It's also a good way to use up any leftover meat sitting in the refrigerator. I've made it with ham, chicken, turkey, pork roast, salmon, and even tempeh.

Bring stock to a boil in a stockpot over medium-high heat, add dried vegetables, remove from heat, cover, and let sit for 1 hour.

Return pot to medium heat and simmer, stirring occasionally, for 2 hours. Add meat and simmer another 4 minutes. Season to taste with salt and pepper. Serve immediately.

Vegetable Stock

**Yield: approximately
2 litres**

----

6 cups mixed,
    roughly chopped
    fresh vegetables
10 peppercorns
2 bay leaves
2 teaspoons Herb
    Salt (see *page 220*)
2 litres water

Basic, flexible, and delicious, I use this for everything. I like to include onion, carrot or parsnip, and celery or fennel in the vegetable mix whenever possible. Avoid using leafy greens.

Combine all ingredients in a large stockpot. Bring just to a simmer over medium-low heat. Continue to simmer until vegetables are very tender, about 3 hours.

Remove large chunks with a slotted spoon, then strain remaining liquid through cheesecloth or a mesh bag. Stock will keep in the refrigerator for 3 days or the freezer for 2 months.

Berry Maritime Rumtopf

Yield: approximately 8 quarts

½ pound stemmed, sliced strawberries

½ pound raspberries

½ pound blueberries

½ pound pitted, stemmed cherries

½ pound pitted, chopped plums

½ pound pitted, chopped peaches

½ pound cored, chopped apples (any varietal; I like a combination of Honeycrisp and Orange Cox's Pippin)

½ pound cored, chopped pears

4 cups sugar, divided

6 cups light or dark rum, divided

Rumtopf is a traditional German dish that is made throughout the summer and fall and served at Christmastime. It's one of my favourite ways to preserve the best of seasonal fruits throughout the growing season, and it makes an impressive and attractive present. The fruits listed here are suggestions, but you can really substitute any fresh fruit. Make a customized rumtopf with fruit from your garden, or one that showcases the varietals you consider to be particularly outstanding in a given year.

Add each fruit, in season, beginning with strawberries. Layer fruit in one large, clean glass container or evenly across several small ones.

Add ½ cup sugar and ¾ cup rum to each pound of fruit, layering fruit up through apples and pears at the end of the season. Cover mixture tightly after each addition and store in a cool, dark place.

After finishing rumtopf, allow to marinate until the beginning of winter in late December, then enjoy the concentrated sunlight stored in the fruit and sugar to balance out the dark days of the winter solstice.

Seasonal Availability by Produce Type

The following guide lists average availability for produce in the Maritimes. Keep in mind that windows of availability vary depending on weather and a host of other factors. The ideal time to buy in bulk changes from year to year. The best way to gauge which week you should buy that flat of strawberries or barrel of potatoes is to have a conversation with the farmer. Usually it's smack-dab in the middle of its range of availability as listed below, but sometimes it's closer to the end.

Produce	April	May	June	July	Aug.	Sept.	Oct.	Nov.
Apples					●———	———	——●	
Asparagus		●———	——●					
Beans, green					●———	——●		
Beans, mature						●———	——●	
Beets				●———	———	———	——●	
Blackberries					●—●			
Blueberries				●———	———	——●		
Broccoli				●———	———	———	——●	
Brussels sprouts						●———	———	——●
Cabbage				●———	———	———	——●	
Carrots			●———	———*year-round in a cold frame*———				——●
Cauliflower						●———	——●	
Cherries, sour				●—●				
Cherries, sweet			●———	——●				
Corn					●———	——●		
Cranberries							●———	——●
Cucumber					●———	——●		
Eggplant					●———	——●		
Garlic scapes			●———	——●				
Garlic bulbs (fresh)					●———*year-round, cured*——●			
Greens	●———	———	———*year-round in a cold frame*——— (most greens turn bitter in the hot months of July and August)				——●	

Produce	April	May	June	July	Aug.	Sept.	Oct.	Nov.
Onions, green		●————————————————●						
Herbs (outdoors)		●——————— year-round indoors ———————●						
Leeks					●—————————●			
Lettuce		●——— with generally better quality in the cooler months ———●						
Melons					●————●			
Mushrooms	●——————————————— year-round —————————————————●							
Onions (fresh)					●——— year-round, cured ———●			
Parsnips							●————●	
Pears					●—————————●			
Peas			●————————●					
Peppers					●————●			
Plums						●———●		
Potatoes					●—————————●			
Radishes		●————————————————●						
Raspberries				●——————————●				
Rhubarb	●——————————●							
Summer squash				●——————————●				
Strawberries			●————●					
Tomatoes				●——————————●				
Turnips and Rutabagas							●————●	
Winter squash						●—————————●		

Local Produce Sources in the Maritimes

The business of producing food is a dynamic one—every year old farmers retire, and new ones begin their farming adventures. Local markets begin, and established farms launch CSAs. Luckily, there are several terrific organizations in the Maritimes that track local food sources and organize up-to-date information in online databases. Here's a listing of the most comprehensive and reputable sites:

ACORN Organic database of farmers, retailers, farmers' markets, community gardens, CSAs, and more:
acornorganic.org/acorn/databaseregional.html

Community-Supported Agriculture: The CSA Guide for Atlantic Canada:
acornorganic.org/pdf/CSAmanual.pdf

Conservation Council of New Brunswick's listing of local food sources in New Brunswick, including CSAs, Farm Stands, Farmers' Markets, and more:
conservationcouncil.ca/local-food

Farmers' Markets of Nova Scotia website, with up-to-date market information for the entire province:
Farmersmarketsnovascotia.ca/find-a-market

PEI Flavours, a website with a Fresh Products Directory for the Island and more in-depth information about food and products:
peiflavours.ca

Select Nova Scotia website, with a database of local products and where to purchase them:
selectnovascotia.ca

Index

Page numbers in bold refer to recipes